NOAH'S ARK: FOUND

Ron Wyatt

edited and revised
Mary Nell Wyatt Lee, Editor

Published by TREASURED TRUTHS PUBLISHING
Shelbyville, Tennessee

Treasured Truths Publishing
P. O. Box 2221
Shelbyville, Tennessee 37162

ronwyatt.com

Illustrations by Mary Nell (Wyatt) Lee and Ron Wyatt
Photos from the Ron Wyatt Archives

Table of Contents

INTRODUCTION

In 1989, two years after Noah's Ark was officially recognized by Turkey, Ron Wyatt's "Discovered: Noah's Ark" was published. In 1999, Ron passed away. Recently, Ron's daughter, Michelle Wyatt Schelles, and her husband Dennis told me they wanted to reprint "Discovered: Noah's Ark". We decided to take the opportunity to revise it and include more information and photographs.

It has now been 27 years since the Turkish authorities recognized the discovery of Noah's Ark and through the years, it has been visited by people from all over the world. Tour buses still make the treacherous drive up the mountain road to take groups to the Visitor's Center built by the government in 1988. There are even plans to build a larger Visitors Center expected to begin any day now.

In May of 2013 I was there with a tour group and I realized then the importance of making available a book explaining the remains of Noah's Ark because it doesn't look like many people expect it to look. While I was there, a group from South Korea came to Noah's Ark and the Visitor's Center and looked around. Even though we didn't speak the same langauge, I could tell they didn't understand what they were looking at. Pulling out my Ipad, I showed them photos and diagrams, (many that are in this book) and with the help of one man who spoke faltering English, I was able to help them understand by pointing out features. The look of excitement on their faces was worth the trip for me.

It is our hope that by revising Ron's first book about his work on Noah's Ark, that we can reach a new audience- a new generation. The implications of this discovery are serious. If Noah's Ark is real, then the Bible is true. If the Bible is true, then we need to reevaluate our relationship with God, our Creator and our Saviour. That was the sole motivating factor for Ron Wyatt.

Mary Nell (Mrs. Ron Wyatt) Lee

FOREWORD

Many controversies have persisted over the years; some are trivial, and some border on the ridiculous, but some are profound, affecting the very foundations of our beliefs. Those with the most far-reaching and persistent potentials concern the ancient history of mankind as presented in the Holy Bible.

I want to share with you the discovery of Noah's Ark. However, shortly after I became convinced of the authenticity of the Ark, I was divinely guided to several other discoveries which are equally astounding; confirmations of the total infallibility of the Bible. These great treasures, preserved by the Hand of God, I believe, are God's great "attention getters" for those who have been discouraged in total belief in the Word of God.

I first became interested in Noah's Ark in 1960 after reading an article in Life Magazine about a "mysterious boat-shaped object" photographed near Mt. Ararat. By 1975, I knew I was going to see this formation for myself. I believed it was possibly the remains of Noah's Ark.

In 1960, an expedition from the United States went to examine the object and returned after two days of research at the site with the verdict that it was a natural geological formation. There was nothing of any archaeological interest there.

In 1977, I made the first of 25 (to date) trips to Turkey, and after that first trip, I knew for sure; but gaining the evidence needed to convince the world was another matter.

Today, I can say without a doubt the Bible is the inspired Word of God and is a historically accurate and reliable guide to the future.

RONALD E. WYATT

ARCHAEOLOGY

FROM THE AIR the ship-shaped outline lies in the center of a landslide on the slope of a mountain that is only 25 miles from the Russian border. The landslides are of recent origin, may have packed thick mud and stones around the strange form. The photo was shot by a Turkish aerial survey plane from 10,000 feet.

NOAH'S ARK?

Boatlike form is seen near Ararat

While routinely examining aerial photos of his country, a Turkish army captain suddenly gaped at the picture shown above. There, on a mountain 20 miles south of Mt. Ararat, the biblical landfall of Noah's Ark, was a boat-shaped form about 500 feet long. The captain passed on the word. Soon an expedition including American scientists set out for the site.

At 7,000 feet, in the midst of crevasses and landslide debris, the explorers found a clear, grassy area shaped like a ship and rimmed with steep, packed-earth sides. Its dimensions are close to those given in Genesis: "The length of the ark shall be 300 cubits, the breadth of it 50 cubits, and the height of it 30 cubits," that is, 450x75x45 feet. A quick two-day survey revealed no sign that the object was man made. Yet a scientist in the group says nothing in nature could create such a symmetrical shape. A thorough excavation may be made another year to solve the mystery.

1
THE SEARCH IS OVER

On June 20, 1987, a group of Turkish government officials and scientists, a film crew from the United States, and an American archaeologist were gathered on a mountain side in the ancient kingdom of Urartu in eastern Turkey. The purpose of this gathering was the dedication of the area as a national park. The area seemed wild and remote; one had the feeling he was thousands of miles from civilization and thousands of years into the past. As shepherds guided their herds through the craggy mountains, the villagers went about their daily lives in stone dwellings reminiscent of a bygone era. The rolling mountains dominated the vast countryside which was broken by towering spires of stone that betrayed the seismic violence that had dominated the region at the dawn of civilization.

Then as one turned and lifted his gaze, the lofty grandeur of the cloud-enshrouded Agri Dagh (Ararat) filled the northern sky. This mystical mountain had for millennia spawned many grandiose and tragic legends of the abodes of the gods and the refuge of the survivors of a world devastated by a universal flood.

As the ceremony began, the guest of honor turned for a moment to gaze upon Agri Dagh's compelling beauty and marveled as she seemed to pull her veil of clouds about her as a shroud. It was as if the mountain herself knew her deception had been revealed. A tear welled in his eye and found its way down his weathered face as he thought of the countless millions of human kind who had been and were still being swept to destruction by demon-inspired deceptions. These cunningly devised fables had been enthusiastically received from lying lips by those who loved not the truth. Millions had and will continue to pay dearly for "loving and believing a lie."

The dedication of Noah's Ark National Park was festive. The government officials were delighted with the prospects of the influx of tourists and of more money with which to improve the lives of their people. The locals were happy with the good jobs made available through the construction of the new highway leading to the visitor's center soon to be built overlooking the remains of Noah's Ark. The military officials were happily contemplating their responsibilities of providing safety for the countless visitors. The film crew was happily filming the joyous occasion while thoughts of fame and fortune danced through their minds. Ron Wyatt's silent tears of relief from years of opposition and struggle went unnoticed amid the mirth of the day.

Front page of "Hurriyet", dated 21 Harizan 1987 (June 21, 1987): by Ibrahim Ozturk

Nuhun Gemisi turizme açıldı

● Doğubeyazıt İlçesi'nin Üzengili Köyü yakınlarındaki gemiye benzer toprak yığınının çevresi "milli park" haline getiriliyor.

İbrahim ÖZTÜRK

D OĞUBEYAZIT,(hha)- Doğubeyazıt İlçesine bağlı Üzengili Köyü yakınlarında bulunan gemiye benzer toprak yığınının Nuh'un Gemisi olduğu ABD'li bilim adamlarınca da doğrulandı. Geminin bulunduğu saha milli park olarak ilan edildi ve turizme açıldı.

Doğubeyazıt'a 15 kilometre uzaklıkta bulunan Üzengili Köyü'nde Türk bilim adamlarından sonra ABD'li araştırmacı Wyatt Ronolt Eldon ile beraberindeki 5 kişi de araştırmalar yaptı. Toprağın yapısı bulunan demir parçalardan Nuh'un Gemisi'nin Üzengili'de olduğu ABD'li araştırmacılar tarafından da doğrulandı.

Ağrı Valisi Şevket Ekinci, Doğubeyazıt Kaymakamı Cengiz Gökçe, Belediye Başkanı Osman Baydar, yerli ve yabancı bilim adamlar ile yurttaşların katıldığı törenle Nuh'un Gemisi'nin bulunduğu alan turizme açıldı. Vali Şevket Ekinci, "Son yıllarda Türkiye, dünya turizminde aranan ülkelerden biri haline gelmiştir. Kur'an-ı Kerim ve İncil'de adı geçen Nuh'un Gemisi'nin burada olduğu kesinlik kazanmıştır. Dünyada milyonların dikkatini üzerine çeken Nuh'un Gemisi'nin bulunduğu alanı turizme açmaktan kıvanç duyuyorum. Geminin bulunmasında emeği geçen yerli ve yabancı bilim adamlarına teşekkür borçluyuz. Burada yapacağımız sosyal tesislerde, yerli ve yabancı turistleri ağırlayacak ve ülkemize döviz kazandıracağız"dedi.

NOAH'S ARK AREA IS OPENING TO TOURISM

DOGUBEYAZIT,(hha) - At the Uzengili village, which is near the Dogubeyazit district is located the boat-shaped formation. Scientists from the U.S.A. have confirmed that it is Noah's Ark. The governor has announced that it is now a national park and open for tourists.

At Uzengili village, which is 15 kilometers from Dogubeyazit, Turkish scientists, Mr. Ronald Eldon Wyatt and his team from the U.S.A. made a research of the area. They took samples of the soil. Test results revealed that the soil has iron and fossil boat structures. Scientists confirmed that Noah's Ark is at the Uzengili village.

Mr. Sevket Ekinci, Governor of Agri; Mr. Cengiz Gokce, Head Official of the District of Dogubeyazit; Mr. Osman Baydar, President of the Municipality; some Turkish scientists, and Mr. Wyatt participated in the ceremony opening the area for tourists. Mr. Sevket Ekinci said, "Turkey is a country of great interest for tourists. The Holy Bible and the Koran also say that Noah's Ark is in this area." Mr. Ekinci added, "It is my pleasure that I am opening this area which is getting great attention for Noah's Ark and I appreciate all the scientists for discovering Noah's Ark. We are laying a foundation for a welcome center for Turkish and foreign tourists. Thank you."

June 20, 1987: The Dedication Ceremony of Noah's Ark with guest-of-honor, Ron Wyatt

13

Top- A meal at the dedication with the ark seen behind (above right in the photo.)
Below- The Governor requests all Turkish degnitaries to the ark where, in the presence of Turkish Radio and Television (TRT) he has Ron demonstrate the radar.
Next page top- Ron demonstrating subsurface interface radar for the dignitaries.
Next page bottom- Gov. of Agri, Sevket Ekinci, congratulates Ron Wyatt.

15

The Erzurum Hotel in Dogubeyazit, Turkey looking out the window onto the roof where Ron and his sons stayed in August of 1977.

2
THE YEARS OF RESEARCH
1977 - 1987

The night was hot and sultry in eastern Turkey; the heat and darkness seemed like co-conspirators with the danger exploding just outside our door...

"Ronny! Are you awake? We've gotta get outta here! Some of those villagers are trying to kill us!"

My younger son, Ronny, was 15 at the time and had been sleeping in room 303 of the Erzurum Hotel in Dogubeyazit. My other son, Danny, then 17, and I were across the hall in room 308. When we heard the pummeling of heavily shod feet rushing up the stairs, I shouted commands for the boys to grab what they could and get into the room Ronny was in, which had a window that opened above the back roof. The window in our room had a fire escape of sorts, and we'd be sitting ducks if we stayed in there.

We grabbed what we could and barricaded ourselves in room 303 by shoving the bed against the door and pushing the chest between the bed and the wall. Little was spoken as our minds raced, trying to comprehend what was happening to us. We could hear the attempted use of a passkey in the lock as the door appeared to strain against the weight of the angry mob just outside, threatening to disintegrate and loose upon us the furious knot of assailants. Our mouths and throats were excruciatingly dry from the lack of safe drinking water and also from the rush of adrenaline propelled into our systems. Desperately, our minds cast about for any means of escape, and I wondered how my well-laid plans had deteriorated to this.

That scenario took place during my first trip to Turkey in 1977, and it was that trip which provided me with the discoveries that proved to me the boat-shaped object I was in search of was indeed the remains of Noah's Ark. It would be another ten years of painstaking and costly research before the Turkish government was convinced the boat was real, but today the evidence is in. Today, there is a Visitor's Center just above the ark where visitors from all over the world come to see this most amazing discovery.

During the summer of 1977, my two sons and I found ourselves at risk in a strange country amongst a people of strange speech. They attempted to rob and possibly kill us. (For the record, the same thing could and often does happen to tourists who visit our country and fall among the criminal element of our society.) This "nervousing experience", (a term coined by my youngest son, Ronny, that fit the situation), was the beginning of many years of slow, meticulous, frustrating research that culminated in undeniable proof of the reality and location of the remains of Noah's Ark.

Our first trip to eastern Turkey produced a veritable landslide of discoveries and excitement and set the pace for a breathtakingly rapid sequence of discoveries that left us in a state of mind that had us mentally "pinching ourselves" from the difficulty of accepting the reality of it all.

Our discoveries on that trip included several massive, pierced drogue stones that bore an eight-cross iconographic representation of the eight survivors of the flood. These crosses were inscribed by the Byzantine and Crusader Christians, which proved that something or someone convinced them that these pierced stones were relics from Noah's Ark.

Below- Danny (left) and Ronny (right) in 1977.

Massive Drogue-Style Anchorstones

  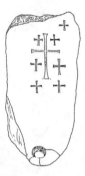 

Drawings by Mary Nell Wyatt (Lee), at left seen with Ron as she sketches.

Ron in 1979 by drogue stone.

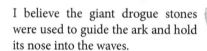

I believe the giant drogue stones were used to guide the ark and hold its nose into the waves.

Ron by one of the large drogue stones.

Marty Plott by a drogue from the Mediterranean Sea showing the much smaller size of later drogue stones.

20

We found two grave markers that bore the eight-cross symbols of Noah and his family above an ancient petroglyphic portrayal of Noah's death on one marker and that of his wife on the other. These grave markers were in the front of a very ancient stone house, seen below.

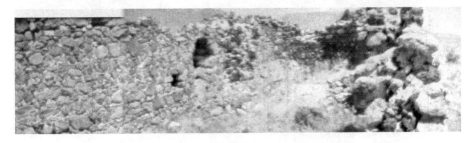

These markers and the house have been vandalized, and over one hundred million U.S. dollars worth of gold and gemstones were stolen from the graves. The Turkish authorities are seeking to recover these precious artifacts and to punish the thieves. At present, they are aware of the identity of the most probable person responsible for this outrage, but he disappeared from the public eye shortly after the theft from Noah's and his wife's graves. (Update- As of the present, 2014, nothing further has been done to apprehend whoever took these items nor have any of them been recovered).

In the above photo, taken from movie film, one tombstone can be seen in 1977. In the photo below , also from movie film, a petroglyph of a wave with a ship atop the wave, to Ron, was an obvious reference to the ark and the flood.

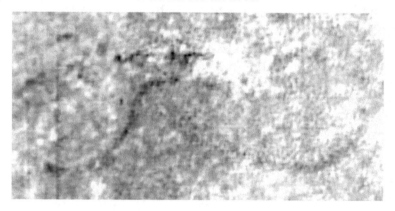

We located and photographed several other inscriptions and physical remains of the flood and the Ark. We got a brief look at the boat remains before we were forced to flee for our lives. Upon our arrival back in the states, we had our super-eight movie film developed and were delighted to see that we had good photographic documentation of all the artifacts and inscriptions.

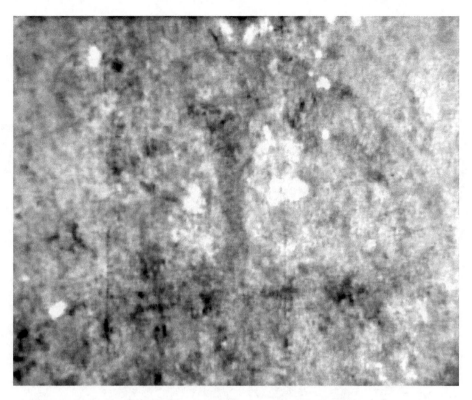

Closeup of the top of the tombstone showing a rainbow across the top. A large cross has been superimposed on the original inscription.

Shortly after our return, a friend called to inform me that an M.D. PhD, Dr. William Shea, from a university in Michigan had written several articles that stated his belief that the boat formation was related to the landing site of Noah's Ark. I contacted Dr. Shea and shared our discoveries with him. He was delighted, reviewed the inscriptions, recognized the pierced drogue stones as probable relics from the Ark and joined with me in applying to the Turkish government for permission to excavate the boat-shaped formation. The Turkish authorities declined to give us a permit at that time. We got the same reply after a second request; we were stymied.

My sons and I spent the summer of 1978 locating and documenting the site where Moses and the Hebrew slaves crossed the Red Sea. Yet, all the while, we were unable to forget the fantastic discoveries associated with Noah's Ark.

We, with some trusted friends, prayed that God would see fit to send an earthquake that would in some manner expose the boat formation for what it was without injury to any of the inhabitants of the area. Watching the evening news in late 1978, I was thrilled to see that an earthquake had hit the area where the Ark remains were located and that there had been no casualties. I made arrangements to return to the site, and arrived there in the early summer of 1979.

Above- Ron's 1979 photo of the object after the earthquake.

Photo of the site prior to the earthquake.

The formation had been split down the middle along its entire length, and the earth had fallen away from its sides. This allowed me to take clean, fresh samples from five locations along the center and sides of the boat. It also made it possible to carefully measure the depth of the object along its length and to document the dimensions of several of the main structural timbers that were exposed.

I photographed the formation and its exposed structures and returned home with a veritable treasure-trove of archaeological data and specimens.

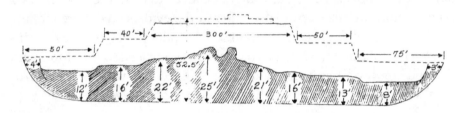

Diagram of Ron's original measurements taken in 1979 showing the depth of the material, the length and how the location of each level, or deck, can be determined by the changing thickness of the deposit.

Galbraith Laboratories of Knoxville, Tennessee was highly recommended, and I entrusted the care and analysis of these precious samples to them. The results were astounding. The raw carbon content showed the object to be composed of decayed wood and a high concentration of oxidized metal was shown. We had taken three samples from the site at distances that guaranteed them to be out of the geological influence of the boat remains. These compared favorably with chemical values of normal countryside and proved that the boat formation was composed of decayed and oxidized archaeological remains.

I shared this data with Bill Shea, and on the strength of this evidence, we made reapplication to the Turkish authorities and were again put off. Dr. Shea and I decided that the high metallic contents of the formation warranted evaluation (investigation) with metal detection devices. I contacted Whites Electronic Corporation of Sweet Home, Oregon and was supplied with their best-quality metal detection equipment in 1983.

During the fall of 1983 I became aware that Colonel James Irwin of High Flight Foundation, located in Colorado Springs, Colorado, was searching for the remains of Noah's Ark. I contacted him by phone and was invited to visit him and to share the details of our research with him. He was intrigued by our research and wanted to see the boat formation and also possibly work with us on the investigation and documentation of the Red Sea crossing site, pyramid building, and the Ark of the Covenant. He, his wife Mary, and their family are wonderful friends, and we have highly valued their friendship.

It was Colonel Irwin, I firmly believe, who helped get my sons and me out of prison in Saudi Arabia where we had been mistakenly accused of being Israeli spies in 1984. We had entered the country illegally to hunt for the Biblical Mt. Sinai which I believed to be in the Jebel el Lawz range. Before we were arrested, we found the evidence we were looking for, which included the large altar, the twelve pillars of stone, the remains of a twelve columned, white marbled shrine, dedicated to the "Mountain Of God" (Yahweh) and the altar to the golden calf with twelve petroglyphs of Hathor and Apis, the Egyptian cow and bull gods.

Ron with Col. Jim Irwin in Turkey.

In August, 1984, accompanied by Colonel Jim Irwin and armed with the deep probe metal detectors courteously provided by Whites Electronics, we returned to the boat formation. In the company of Colonel Irwin, Marvin Steffins, Bulant Atalay, "Whatcha" McCullum, a military escort and a Turkish army officer, Orhan Basar, I demonstrated a pattern of metals and/or their oxides that showed the outline of a boat in the formation. The army officer, under my direction, took several small samples from metal brackets and petrified timbers.

1984 photo of Bulant Atalay, Marv Steffins and Ron with the ark in the background.

Mr. Steffins called a news conference a few days later, displayed some bags of specimens "from Noah's Ark", and claimed the discovery. This triggered an international "incident" that resulted in my being accused of stealing archaeological treasures from Turkey by Ted Koppel on "Nightline" the night of August 27, 1984. A call to the Turkish mission at the U.N. led to my exoneration by the Minister of Culture and Tourism, Mukerrem Tascioglu, in an AP interview on August 30, 1984.

When the incident blew over, we proceeded with the analysis of the samples per agreement with the Turkish authorities. The results of these analyses confirmed those taken in 1979 and proved that the formation contained a massive, ancient boat that was built of very large wood-

27

en timbers held in place by many metal brackets and spikes.

In early 1985 I received calls from David Fasold, a specialist in old boat research and identification, and John Baumgardner, PhD., a geophysicist from Los Alamos National Laboratories. I invited them to accompany me to the site later in the year. David introduced the Molecular Frequency Generator into the research, and along with the equipment from Whites Electronics, the resulting surveys identified the massive structure of a boat enclosed within the boat formation.

Ron, John Baumgardner and David Fasold in 1985.

During July/August of 1985, with financial assistance arranged by Dr. Baumgardner and accompanied by David Fasold, John Baumgardner, Tom Anderson, Maylon Wilson, Tom Thaxton, Tom Jarriel, Jim Burroughs, Niel Richline, George House, Judith Moses (ABC's 20/20 producer) and others, we arrived in Dogubeyazit. I had a permit for electronic surveys and those included on my permit from the Turkish government were: David Fasold, John Baumgardner, Normajean Baumgardner, Thomas Anderson, Todd Fisher, Scott Snider, William Shea, Fredrich Bach, Klaus Wattenbach and Zafer Akcay.

We planned to scan the formation with a subsurface interface radar system. This system was developed by Geophysical Survey Systems, Inc. of Hudson, New Hampshire and was accompanied by their geologist, Tom Fenner. The preliminary survey of the site progressed smoothly.

We were accompanied by a group of 30 Turkish Commando who hid in the surrounding countryside for our protection. Turkish intelligence had informed me that an attempt would likely be made to kidnap or kill Colonel Irwin and/or myself; and it turned out that the threat was real. The attack made by some Iranian terrorists resulted in the deaths of five terrorists and three Turkish soldiers. Martial law was declared in the area, our plans were trashed and the radar scan waited until later that fall.

On the next expedition, we surveyed the site with three types of metal detectors and two subsurface radar systems. This data, along with core drilling samples, proved beyond any doubt that a very large (515 feet long), very ancient ship lies within the formation.

During the metal detectors scans of 1985, a pattern of metal readings was detected that was clearly not random. After marking each reading with a rock, they connected the ribbons which revealed the distinct shape of a ship.

Ron and John Baumgardner performing the metal detector scans.

30

3

SUMMARY OF
THE EVIDENCES

The Turkish government has meticulously observed and kept records of the activities and claims of all who have looked for Noah's Ark over the last 50 years. They followed our research step by step and became convinced of the reality of the remains of Nu'hun Gemisi (Noah's Ark) buried within the boat formation.

1. The formation was positively identified as a boat by a number of skilled photogrammetry experts from a set of aerial photographs. In a quote from Rene Noorbergen's book "The Ark File", Dr. Arthur Brandenburger, professor of photogrammetry at Ohio State in Columbus, Ohio, after careful study of the photo of the site stated, *"I have no doubt at all that this object is a ship. In my entire career I have never seen an object like this on a stereo photo."*

Dr. Brandenburger went on the 1960 expedition to the site, but after the team returned home with the verdict that there was nothing there of any archaeological interest, he was still not convinced. In further quotes from the above book, he says later, *"Our measurements in the field verify our laboratory findings. In my opinion further study of this peculiar symmetrical phenomenon should be made by an expert in tectonics."*

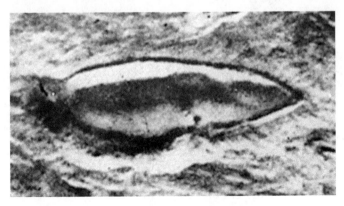

He continued, "*Meanwhile, I have received my developed colored slides of the ship-shaped formation, and I still must say it is an amazing feature. It is doubtless a mystery, and I come always more to the conclusion that our official statement to the press was too negative. The interpretation of the formation is of utmost difficulty, and I am not anymore so sure that, from a serious scientific standpoint, a sole surface archaeological investigation of only two days entitles us to state that the formation is not the ark.*"

2. Twelve years of electronic and mechanical probing has positively identified it as a boat.

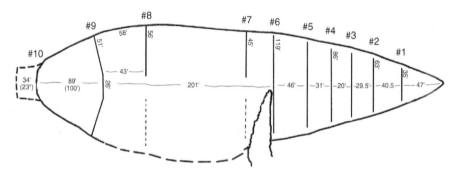

The first radar scans (above diagram) revealed bulkheads and structure deep within the formation. These scans matched with the first metal detector lines obtained in 1984 by myself. I originally recorded 12 metal lines but subsequent scans showed 13 across the width of the ship.

The section below labeled "distorted" is the result of the ship being impaled on a massive outcropping of limestone bedrock as it slid down the mountainside at some unknown point in time. That section is damaged but amazingly shows a metal detector pattern totally consistent

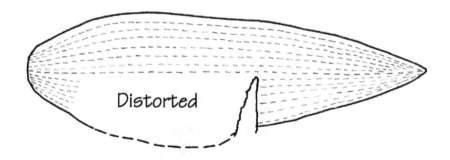

Distorted

with an object being wracked, such as a car "wrapped around" a telephone pole after an accident. See the below photo which shows the very defined area of impalement.

The metal detector surveys showed the deformed area where the ark was impaled by the limestone outcropping which held it at its present location.

3. Samples of petrified wood have been located and taken from the structure in the presence of many witnesses. The most impressive to date was found during the dedication ceremony when I demonstrated the subsurface interface radar for the Turkish dignitaries. I saw a reflection on the radar printout and pointed it out to the Governor, who ordered it to be dug up. Closeup is below.

The below photo is a closeup of the reflection I pointed out. A larger section of that printout is on the following page.

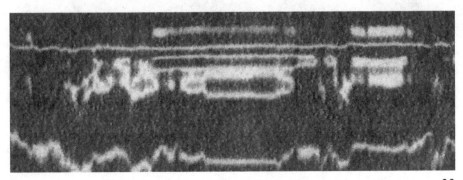

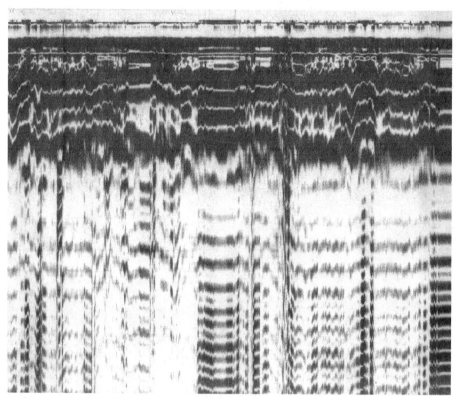

Radar printout showing the reflection of an object top center. Below is the specimen that was found upon digging. Photo on the left shown face up and on right, side that was facing down.

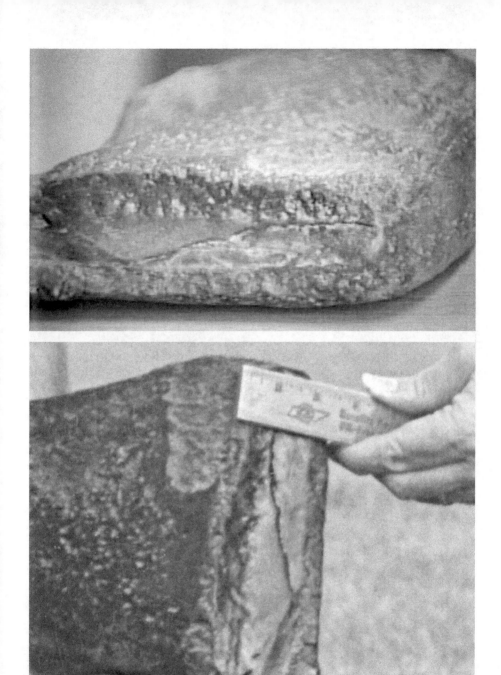

35

There are 2 square metal sites on the "deck timber" specimen. Ron's theory is that when the wood was layered with glue between the layers, small "nails" were inserted to hold the layers in place until the glue (bitumen) dried.

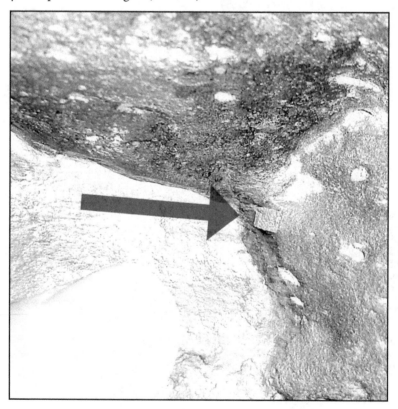

When the specimen was sectioned, it showed what appeared to be at least 5 layers of petrified wood, like our laminated wood or plywood.

Ron posing by the hole where the "deck timber" specimen was found, taken one year later in 1988.

Radar verified the lengthwise metals lines I had found in 1984, then duplicated and refined in 1985 and 1986 with the involvement of a large group of researchers.

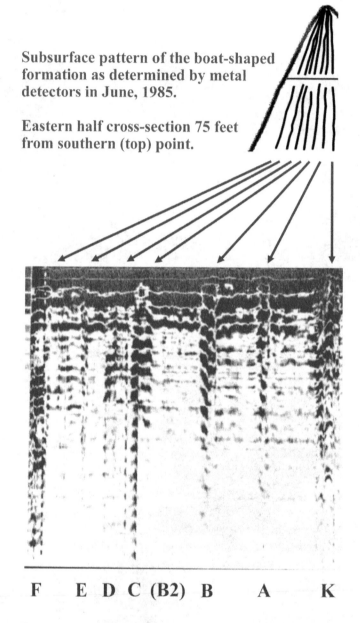

Subsurface pattern of the boat-shaped formation as determined by metal detectors in June, 1985.

Eastern half cross-section 75 feet from southern (top) point.

F   E D C (B2) B   A   K

Subsurface pattern of the boat-shaped formation as determined from Radar scan No. 5 in July, 1986. Eastern half cross-section 75' from southern point.

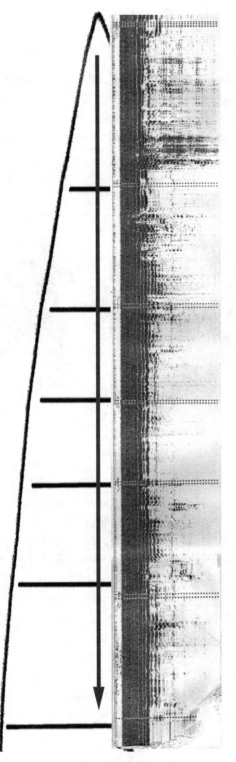

The metal lines that ran from side to side were also verified by radar. The radar notated with dotted lines the strongest reflections.

4. Repeated chemical analysis of many different samples, taken at different times by different people and analyzed at different laboratories, positively prove it to be composed of very ancient wood and metal.

Some early specimens that I retrieved from the ark were taken from the lower end where I spotted a mass of material falling out from the central area. You can see the material in the photo below taken in 1985. Analysis showed this material to be tailings of metal production.

1985 photo showing the ballast material extruding from the lower end of the ark.

In 1984, I gave a specimen to former astronaut, Col. James Irwin and asked him to have it tested. He sent it to Los Alamos National Labs where physicist, Dr. John Baumgardner had it analyzed. On the very detailed analysis he noted, "tailings of aloid production". The semi-quantitative analysis of this specimen showed extremely high levels of MNO, or manganese, the highest being 87.26%, with others at 80.64% and 60.8%. Of interest was the fact that it also contained AL203, or aluminum oxide, as high as 27% in one location and titanium as high as 74.26% in another location.

This specimen resulted in Dr. Baumgardner's interest in the site. I was told by a member of the 1985 team that accompanied Dr. Baumgardner that the reason he was so interested in the site was due to the advanced nature of the specimen; he thought perhaps a satellite had crashed out here somewhere and I mistook it for Noah's Ark.

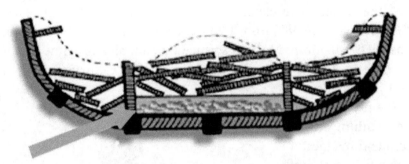

The importance of this material, that I believe to be ballast material, cannot be overestimated. A ship of any size has to have ballast to maintain the stability of the ship in the water. This is a given. But also of great importance is the composition of the material- it is slag (tailings) or waste product of metal production.

What this implies is that the metal objects used in building the ship were made onsite as the ship was being built. As the objects were made, the slag was put into the hull until it was full. This gave Noah and his family a ready supply of certain metals to use after the flood.

The metal readings obtained from the metal detector scans proved there were high concentrations of metals at symmetrical intervals. In 1985, Dr. Baumgardner found a specimen he determined to be "wrought iron" which proved to be 91.84% FE_2O_3.

Right- Dr. Baumgardner holding the wrought iron "angled bracket".

Right- Fossilized rivet found in 1991 that had fallen off the ark.

In 1991,we found a most amazing specimen which gave us more insight into the fittings used in the construction of the massive ship. This object at once displayed the appearance of a rivet.

The quantitative elemental analyses of the rivet-head revealed 8.62% aluminum, 10.38% iron, 1.33% magnesium, and 2.7% sodium, as well as 1.92% titanium. Modern science was not able to refine titanium intil 1936. Yet, here is a fossilized specimen with elements of very advanced metal produc-

tion. The process for refining titanium involves sodium and magnesium and the fact that both are present in the analysis of the rivet head is pretty conclusive evidence that Noah and those who helped build this massive ship were far advanced in knowledge of metallurgy.

Right, all photos of the rivet head found in 1991.

Below- diagrams of how they were used on the ark.

5. A number of ancient and medieval inscriptions near the site identify it as Noah's Ark.

In 1979, I found an ancient stele written in an unknown language with a picture carved above the writing. I believe it depicted the mountain ridge above the ark, 2 ravens, and 8 faces (the family of Noah) carved into a boat shape.

I drew the picture as best I could because I was unable to photograph it. We later found it had been broken into pieces and used in a boundary marker by the military base about a mile above the ark.

Sections of the petroglyphs are still visible and we have learned that the broken stones are still there and can hopefully be fully documented.

Above- Ron standing with his driver, Dilaver Avci and 2 soldiers at the broken marker in 1988.

Below- Ron's original drawing of the stele before it was broken.

43

6. Its 515 foot length and its 138 foot width (splayed) are the measure-ments of Noah's Ark as recorded by Moses (educated to use the ancient Egyptian cubit) in the Book of Genesis. See more on this subject in the chapter "Questions I Am Most Frequently Asked About Noah's Ark".

7. It is located in the mountains of Urartu (Ararat) as specified in the Bible. *Gen 8:4 And the ark rested in the seventh month, on the seventeenth day of the month, upon the mountains of Ararat.*

8. Its location at an elevation of 6300 feet above sea level is above any possible height reachable by a "local flood" but is below the maximum water level that would result from all the water of our planet washing the earth's surface (7000-8000 feet).

9. Its location, many miles from any present or ancient body of water that would support it, defies any other explanation.

10. Its massive size and weight make it impossible to "trundle" (drag) this distance from water and its altitude above present and past sea levels defies any other explanation.

11. This writer, in the presence of Turkish authorities and other ob-servers, performed an electronic survey of a similar looking site that some said resembled the boat formation. (The similarities were vague at best). The metal detectors and sub-surface radar scans showed nothing unusual in the site.

12. A careful electronic survey of the area around the formation showed none of the structures present in the formation.

4

QUESTIONS I AM MOST FREQUENTLY ASKED ABOUT NOAH'S ARK

Question 1- The "object" you claim is the remains of Noah's Ark is about 515 feet long and 138 feet wide. The Bible says the Ark was 300 cubits long and 50 cubits wide. I always believed that would mean the Ark would have been 450 feet long by 75 feet wide. How do you explain this discrepancy with the Bible?

Answer- This is one of the most exciting confirmations of the authenticity of the object being the Ark, in my estimation. The Encyclopedia Britannica (1985 edition) states: *"Although there is evidence that many early civilizations devised standards of measurements and some tools for measuring, the Egyptian cubit is generally recognized as having been the most ubiquitous standard of linear measurement in the very ancient world."*

The royal Egyptian cubit was 20.62 inches. If we consider the Biblical statement that Moses was "learned in all the wisdom of Egypt" (Acts 7:22), as the author of Genesis, he would have been referring to the only cubit he knew- the Royal Egyptian Cubit. 300 cubits = 515.5 feet. 50 cubits = 85.9 feet. The measurement of the length of the boat, taken in August, 1985 by Maylon Wilson and John Baumgardner of Los Alamos Laboratory with sophisticated measurement devices, showed the inside length of the boat to be 515.7 feet. David Fasold's measurement of the same was exactly 515 feet.

The width of 138 feet, (my measurement and also David's) may at first seem to present a problem until we consider it carefully. The boat is splayed. The height given in the Bible is 30 cubits or 51.55 feet. The width is given as 50 cubits or 85.916 feet.

The total of both sides plus the width is 189.016 feet -far too wide. But if the hull of the ship was exactly half the entire height of the boat, and the hull splayed outward, the width would be 137.466 feet. Our later metal detection results confirmed these figures as well as the sub-surface interface radar scans.

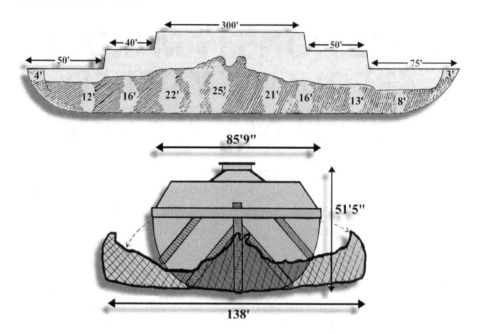

Question 2- I understand that other creationists have stated that what you claim to be petrified wood extending from the formation cannot possibly be wood. Isn't it a simple matter to prove something is petrified wood?

Answer- Yes it is, normally; however, part of the identification of a petrified object is visual. If it looks like a shell, chances are it's a shell. If it looks like wood, then it's wood.

But, there's a problem with this wood- it looks like wood except for one thing- it has no growth rings. If we truly believe the Biblical description of the earth before the flood (Gen. 2:5 and 6), we know that there couldn't possibly be any growth rings in pre-flood wood because there wasn't rain. In "The New Larousse Encyclopedia of the Earth", page 369, we read:

"To support trunks of six-foot base diameter and 60-to 100- foot height, tissues must have increased in thickness from year to year. There was, as we have already said, secondary- bark and wood, similar to that of modern trees but lacking the spring and winter rings which correspond to

seasonal alternation of moisture and dryness."

This is in reference to ancient sigillarias found without any growth rings. But isn't it a pity that I had to go to a book that refers to the earth's age in "millions of years" to find a reference corroborating the fact that these fossils have been found without growth rings? If growth rings were in the wood of the Ark, it would be a fake or replica.

Question 3- What about laboratory testing of samples from the Ark. Have you had this done?

Answer:-Yes, I obtained samples from the boat itself and from the land around the Ark. I had several of these samples tested at Galbraith Labs in Knoxville, Tennessee. Just like medical tests, these results have to be read and interpreted by people trained to do so, so I will quote William Shea, M.D. PhD., Professor of Archaeology and History of Antiquity, in his report to the Turkish government dated February 20, 1987: *"The formation was struck by an earthquake in December of 1978. As a result it was cracked lengthwise and partially split open. This opening made it possible for Wyatt to obtain relatively fresh internal soil samples from it when he returned to the site in September of 1979. In a test run on this sample, along with another sample taken from the field outside of the formation, the organic carbon content was measured. The soil from the formation tested at 4.95% while the soil from the field around the formation tested at 1.88%. This degree of difference is consistent with the prior presence of some organic matter (like wood) in the formation."*

I have had numerous other specimens tested which revealed extremely high metallic contents which caused me to wonder if there might not be metal in the Ark itself. This led to the metal detection testing which revealed the fantastic structure of a massive boat.

Question 4- Explain the metal detection tests and how it could prove any internal structure. Couldn't it just be trace metal in the soil?

Answer- No. On the Ark the metal detecting equipment gave positive readings on its calibrated dial and by sound at numerous points all over the boat. We were able to determine that there was significant amounts of metal present and that it was in a pattern. The testing of the surrounding area was completely negative.

In May of 1985, John Baumgardner and David Fasold, a marine

salvor from Florida, accompanied me to the site, and with the metal detectors and David's new type of metal detector, a molecular frequency generator, we mapped out the metal readings with plastic tapes. It revealed a distinct linear subsurface pattern. We repeated this again in August of 1985, with John Baumgardner and myself accompanied this time by Maylon Wilson, also of Los Alamos Laboratories, and Tom Anderson, a lawyer from Indio, California, who filmed the entire event. We videoed the tests ourselves on both occasions and photographed it thoroughly.

On the outer wall of the boat, striations appear which are keenly visible along the east side of the upper portion and the west side of the lower portion. On the striations, the metal readings were positive while the spaces between were totally negative. In the **photo below**, David Fasold is pointing out the ribbons that show the metal detector readings on the outside hull of the ark.

Question 5- What about the radar scans you mention? What is sub-surface interface radar, and what did the use of it prove?

Answer- Without having to get highly technical, this type of radar works by the generation of an electromagnetic pulse which is radiated into the earth from a broad band width antenna. This pulse can be focused to a particular depth where it is then reflected back and recorded on a graphic recorder similar to an EKG.

48

Quite a sophisticated device, it requires training to operate and to read the results accurately.

I received thorough training at Geophysical Survey Systems, Inc. in Hudson, New Hampshire. The first scan took place in July of 1986. On this expedition were me, Baumgardner and Anderson from the August, 1985 expedition, as well as Mrs. Baumgardner, Dr. William Shea of Andrews University and two cameramen, Todd Fisher and Scott Snider, from Los Angeles. This radar scan confirmed, with astounding detail, the same pattern demonstrated by the metal detectors. Where it was remotely possible to have incorrectly connected the lines resulting from the metal detectors, the radar scan showed what can only be identified as a keel, keelsons and bulkheads from a boat of tremendous size.

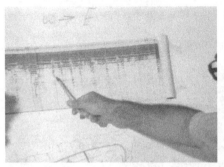

Joe Rosetta, Vice President of Geophysical Survey Systems, Inc., the manufacturer of the radar system, reviewed the scan data and watched the actual scans in progress on video. He went on the record on TV, stating, *"These reflections occur too periodic to be random, natural interfaces.... Some human made this structure, whatever it is."*

49

Question 6- What do the scientists and other experts you have taken to the "boat" say; do they believe it is the Ark?

Answer- Dr. William Shea has worked with me on this from the very beginning. He is a professional in the field of archaeology and ancient history and most open-minded to facts. While I have not a statement from him recently, I will quote from an article he wrote for "Archaeology and Biblical Research", Winter, 1988, entitled "Noah's Ark?" on page 14: *"... The last half of the list point to the general conclusion that the remains*

Dr. William Shea in Turkey examining one of the drogue stones.

of a ship appear to be present in this
formation. The first half are of a more
specific nature that would connect
the remains of such a ship with the
Ark of Noah described in Genesis.
The progressive convergence of these
various lines of evidence seem to con-
firm the conclusion that some of the
remains of Noah's Ark lie within this
unusual formation."

Dr. John Baumgardner
appears to have changed his mind
about what he believes. So as to
avoid misquoting him I will quote from David Fasold's book, "The Ark
of Noah": *"John didn't hear the remark. I think he was off someplace in*
Tubal-cain's foundry five thousand years ago. He held in his hand a piece
of wrought iron, the grain of the stretched and hammered angle bracket still
clearly visible.

It was complete pandemonium after that. Once John knew what
to look for, fittings were all over the place. He could walk down the top
of the wall with the detector going beep,... beep every two or three steps.
Now it was the trained eye of a scientist, looking for things out of place in
the natural covering of the mud, followed by his 'Look at this!' growing in
excitement. I kept the video going as I ran around, stumbling behind him,
then moved to the mound to record his discoveries from a distance to give
perspective to the viewer. No sooner had I left him when he suddenly yelled,
'Undecomposed iron!'

I ran down the mound again and crouched to my knees. I zoomed
in on the mud wall. There, surrounded by the brown matrix of mud, was
a perfectly rectangular beam end of a bluish-gray agglomeration of small
rough stones. The upper and lower right corners were absolutely square,
and projecting from within were what appeared to be iron flakes which had
given the signals."

The results of the analysis on that metal bracket are recorded also
in David's book: *"I hurriedly opened the first-class envelope labeled 'Los*
Alamos National Laboratory.' It contained the semiquantitative analysis of
the iron samples we had recovered from the Ark. The stoichiometric results
were impressive, with the seven running from 60 percent through 91.84 per-
cent FE203. The highest reading was obtained from an angular bracket."

Later we read of a news broadcast which David meticulously recorded: *"Soon there followed daily broadcasts... has this report on what the scientists have found so far... could this be the final resting place of Noah's Ark? ... Dr. John Baumgardner, a geophysicist at the Los Alamos Research Lab in New Mexico... using a metal detector, Baumgardner has been able to confirm the existence of metal at regular intervals. Baumgardner says he believes that metal is at the points where these lines intersect, giving* rise to speculation metal was used in the infrastructure of the craft.'"

Question 7- I don't see how these drogue stones prove it's the Ark. If they are several miles from the site you claim is the Ark, how does that prove anything?

Answer- The drogue stones have tremendous significance in more ways than one. First of all, they are by far the largest drogue (or anchor) stones ever found in the history of the world. The leading authority on anchor stones is considered to be Honor Frost, who in 1973 published, "Ancore, the Potsherd of Marine Archaeology: On the Recording of Pierced Stones from the Mediterranean". Based on her thorough research, we learn that 700 kgs., or 1,543 lbs. is one of the heaviest, if not the heaviest, anchor stone ever found. That is until these. One of the largest I've found is almost 11 feet tall, but the average height is 10 feet by a 5 foot width. David Fasold, in his book, estimates the average weight of these anchor stones to be 8,700 lbs.

To date, there are 13 of these that I have seen. There are several more that I believe to be anchors, but they are partially buried in an upright position and exhibit some of the same characteristics as those we are sure of. Eight of them have the inscriptions which make it evident that some people at some point in time made a direct connection between these and Noah and the Ark. However, some people suggest that whoever carved the crosses probably also carved the drogue stones. I know this is definitely not the case, as when I was at the site in April 1988, I found two more drogue stones which were buried and just barely surfacing for obviously the first time and these did not have any crosses or any other carvings on them.

As for the placement of these drogue stones, it becomes quite evident that as the Ark drifted between two submerged peaks in a ridge of small mountains, the first two drogues snagged and tethered the ship which is likely why Noah removed the covering on the ark and then saw

52

the tops of the mountains. We found a large piece of petrified bark in the same vicinity which I believe to be a portion of that covering.

The petrified bark near the drogue stones in 2013.

He then cut the drogue stones loose, leaving them on the two peaks, a short distance apart. As the boat continued to drift in a direct line through these mountains toward its final resting place, seven more drogues, and probably more, were cut loose and landed near, if not exactly, where they are at present.

The village where five of these are located is in a direct line with the twin peaks of the ridge where the first two dropped. The two that are buried are also in this direct line, and finally about eight miles further, about 1/4 mile below the boat, lies the 10th one.

These drogue stones are far too large to be carried by men. It has been suggested that they aren't drogues at all and that the holes are the means by which they were dragged to their present locations. This is impossible, as the location and size of the holes are such that out of water they would break off under the tremendous stress. Only in the buoyancy of the water could they be held by ropes. Of interest also is the fact that the holes have a larger inner diameter than outer. When the ropes were secured through the holes, knots were tied inside the "scooped-out" hole, and as the water swelled the knotted rope, it was prevented from rubbing and eventually wearing the rope in two from the friction.

The ropehole in one of the drogue stones. Notice how it is hollowed out larger inside.

5

How Was the Ark Preserved?

The ark was preserved because it was covered in lava flow which effectively sealed it and preserved it. The mountain it is on is not volcanic, though. The evidence indicates that the lava resulted from the eruption of a volcano a few miles to the south in present-day Iran.

The lava from that mountain was ejected into the air and carried to the top of the ridge above the ark's present location. It apparently erupted and then collapsed. The lava traveled down the side of the mountain, covering the ark. The path of the lava can be distinctly seen in the present mud-flow area.

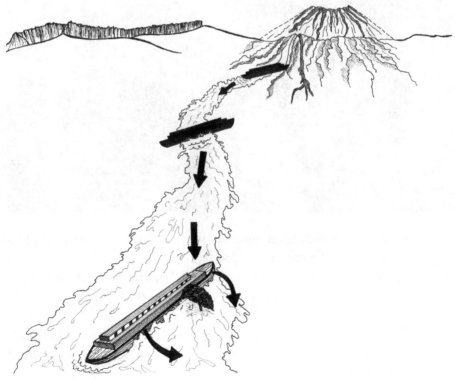

One possible way mud flows are formed is when water is trapped over a long period of time in the slowly decaying lava. Then, when the lava finally deteriorates into soil, the tremendous amount of water captured and retained in it begins to flow, sometimes quite rapidly and catastrophicly, which is called a mud-slide.

When the lava erupted and covered the ark, the weight of this tremendous amount of molten rock flowing upon the ark caused the 2 top decks to collapse. So, why wasn't the ark burned up? There are 2 possibilities as to why it wasn't burned up- the first is this- assuming the lava was the type which would have caused a wooden object to catch on fire, if the ark was completely covered by lava rapidly, this would cut off the oxygen supply and combustion would not be possible.

But, supposing it was covered more slowly, it is a documented fact that lava does not always cause combustion.

"*It might be supposed that the high temperatures of the lava would give off an enormous amount of heat, This is not so, however, and it is quite usual for a flow to pass through a forest or town without causing a fire. One flow from Paricutin even piled up against oaks and cotton-woods without destroying them.... How can we explain this anomaly of high lava temperature and absence of fire and flames? To begin with, lava consists of a vitreous mass which is a poor conductor of heat. It also cools quickly at the surface, becoming covered with a crust which in some measure prevents further heat radiation from inside the mass. Thus a lava flow has, as it were, a constantly forming insulating case around its molten interior, so that the front of the flow is preceded by a protecting crust.*" The New Larousse Encyclopedia of the Earth, pub. by Hamlin Publishing Group Limited, copyrighted 1961, revised edition 1972, page 158.

The fact that the decks seem to be uniformly collapsed indicates that it was covered rapidly, which would have cut off the oxygen supply. We do have specimens which display some burning, but it seems to be very limited in extent.

The lava covered the ark and sealed it in an air-tight capsule. Then... "*The soils which develop from the decomposition of the lavas, cinders and ashes are exceptionally rich in potash, lime and phosphates..... Many districts of the world with a high agricultural population owe the richness of their land to volcanic material.*" ibid., page. 173.

Hawaii is an excellent example of this- their wonderful soil which produces the beautiful exotic flowers we associate with this paradise are a result of the decayed lava, so rich in the nutrients necessary for perfect growth. But, it takes lava a very long time to deteriorate and we cannot know exactly how long the ark was covered. However, over time, as the lava began its deterioration process, it was no longer air-tight.

The ark is situated on a mountain side and it slopes. The front end is at about a 6,350 foot elevation while the lower end is at about the 6,250 foot elevation. The lava deteriorated over time, and being no longer air-tight, it was no longer water-tight. The region experiences several months of snow with the accompanying cold temperatures. In the spring, the snow slowly melts and as it does, the water flows down the mountainside. This means that as the lava began to deteriorate, this water began to flow through the material which covered the ark.

As the water slowly seeped over the preserved structures of the ark, it began to wash away minute particles of the wood and metal fittings of the structure. This took place on a molecular level; molecule by molecule was washed away. But as each molecule broke loose and washed away with the water, it left a hole the exact size of the molecule that had broken loose.

As the water flowed over the structure, some of the molecules it picked up from materials it had passed over prior to arriving at the ark, lodged in the "molecule holes" left in the structure..

The process I am describing is called "petrification", or "mineral replacement". For an object to become petrified, 2 things are ALWAYS required: first, that the object be buried rapidly, and second that it have water flowing through it.

If it is not airtight and has no water flowing over it, it suffers from decay and is not preserved. Evolutionists will be quick to tell you that petrification takes millions of years to occur, but this is simply not the truth. If petrification does not occur at least as rapidly as the decay rate, the object simply decays away.

As the water flowed down the mountain into the soil and then reached the ark, the structure members nearest the top were petrified with molecules of the substances in the earth ABOVE the ark, which were minerals. As the water flowed over the midsection of the ark, it had picked up molecules from the ark structures it had flowed over prior to reaching the midsection. Therefore, it began to be petrified with substances from its own structure in addition to the substances in the soil above it. At least that is what should have occurred if the object really is the ark. And the evidence at the site shows that this IS exactly what happened.

The deck timber obtained from the approximate mid-section of the ship contained over 13% iron- iron which came from the metal fittings of the structure above mid-section.

The majority of molecules involved in the petrification process are molecules from the natural substances in the earth and the lava. The first analyses we had performed on the specimens from the site showed an approximate 51% silica content. That's to be expected as "The Encyclopaedia Brittanica", 1985 ed., vol. 19, page 506, (under "volcanoes") states: " *Magma consists of a molten-silicate mass within the earth, of various composition...*"

In fact, all petrified objects contain a great deal of silica simply due to its abundance in the soil.

But there is one substance that is not found in natural minerals, which I will note. As we study the subject of "carbon", which involves the study of chemistry, we learn some very interesting facts. Compounds of carbon can be analyzed to determine whether they are composed of matter that was non-organic, or organic, which means it can be determined whether they were once living-matter or not. It's that simple. Therefore, the one test to determine if an object was organic (once living), or not is to determine its carbon content- whether it contains organic carbon or not.

When I brought the petrified deck timber home, it looked to me, as well as all who saw it, like a piece of wood turned to stone (petrified). However, looks can be deceiving, so I took it to Galbraith Labs to be analyzed. Chiselling a sample from the specimen (on camera), they analyzed it and found that it did contain inorganic carbon (.0081%). However, it also contained .7019% organic carbon, which is over 100 times more than the amount of inorganic carbon.

Every petrified object ever found that was once living,- tree branch, bone, sea shell, etc.,- will show organic carbon in its analysis. So, the deck timber specimen was once composed of living matter. Since it didn't look like a bone or a shell, we feel pretty confident in stating that it is petrified wood.

So where did the iron in the deck timber specimen come from? In order for there to be such a high percentage of iron in the petrified wood, the water which effected its petrification had to pass over a large amount of iron prior to reaching the petrifying object. The soil above the ark does not contain that much iron. One control specimen taken from the area outside the ark, but within 50 or so yards, revealed a .54% iron and .77% ferric oxide content. If we are to believe that the petrified wood received its iron content from the naturally-occurring iron in the region above the ship, we would have to believe that the entire iron content of the region was gathered up by the waters and deposited ONLY in the petrified wood. In other words, it's impossible.

The large amounts of metals in the petrified wood could only come from one place- from the water passing over a large amount of metal in the ark's structure- metal which we now know composes the thousands of fittings which held the timbers together.

And so the ark remained hidden for many, many years, its presence unknown since its being covered by the lava flow, which incidentally carried it down the mountain until it was impaled on a massive outcropping of bedrock.

In the late 1950's, the high-altitude photo taken during the NATO survey showed this incredible outline of a ship high on a mountainside in a mudflow. The first expedition to the site in 1960 didn't see anything they could recognize as being a man-made object because all that was visible was the decayed lava which was now a layer of rich, fertile soil. Here and there a "rock" protruded through the earth which was actually petrified wood, but its weathered condition camouflaged its true identify. The early expedition didn't understand what to expect- they were looking for an intact boat.

Then, in late 1978, an earthquake caused the soil surrounding the mysterious "shape" to fall away from the sides, giving the effect that the object had literally popped up from the earth. With the soil removed from the sides, the object took on even more of the recognizable shape of a ship. The sides displayed indentions at evenly spaced intervals, which were actually the empty spaces where rib timbers once were. But what happened to the rib timbers if they were petrified? The answer is they are crumbling and falling away due to the effect of weathering.

"Whenever rocks are exposed to attack by weathering process, loose material forms, sometimes in large quantities.... Mass wasting is almost inseparable from weathering and the many other agents of gradation. Water, for example, aids its work considerably.... In mountain areas daily freeze-and-thaw action, or frost wedging, plays its part. Fissures in the rocks fill with water which freezes and expands at night. Under the pressure of the innumerable wedges of ice, the rock cracks. Next morning, the ice melts in the sun and no longer supports the rock fragments, many of which roll down the slope to join other rocks and debris at the foot.". The New Larousse Encyclopedia of the Earth, page 41.

Remember that the structures of the ark were petrified and now turned to stone. When the soil around the sides of the ark was still in place, the ribs were preserved. The way we know is simple- the empty indentations, evenly spaced, are all the evidence we need. Like a footprint in the mud, they wouldn't be there if a foot hadn't been there earlier.

Crumbling exposed rib timbers on the side of the ark.

The weather extremes of the region had accomplished this process of "frost wedging" which fractured the rib timbers which were now turned to stone. They remained in place as long as the surrounding soil held them. But when it fell away, the fractured "turned to stone" timbers fell into pieces and specimens of the petrified wood lie all around the site.

The internal structure members are in a much better state simply because they have not been exposed to the elements. On the east side of the ark is a section in which the rib timbers are exposed but have not completely fallen away and left holes where they once were. However, these ARE fractured, having suffered from "frost wedging". They are still held in place by the soil, probably due to their angle and also some Divine assistance.

We have two specimens of petrified wood, both about 6 inches long, both 2 inches wide and 1 1/2 inches deep. They are identical except for one thing- the piece which came from inside the crack near the front of the ship is very light colored, while the other piece is dark. They are both petrified wood pieces from the ship, only one piece's molecules were replaced by lighter colored substances than the other. Below is the specimen I removed in 1979 from the fresh crack in the ark right after the earthquake.

Petrified wood specimen Ron took from the crack down the ark, on the upper end. It's light color is indicative of the materials that contributed to its petrification.

The timbers which extend out through the ground surface, such as the deck support beams and the deck joists, today look like ordinary rocks. Why? Because they ARE rocks- petrification, or mineral replacement, turns objects into rocks. And these petrified timbers have been exposed to the elements and have suffered extreme weathering.

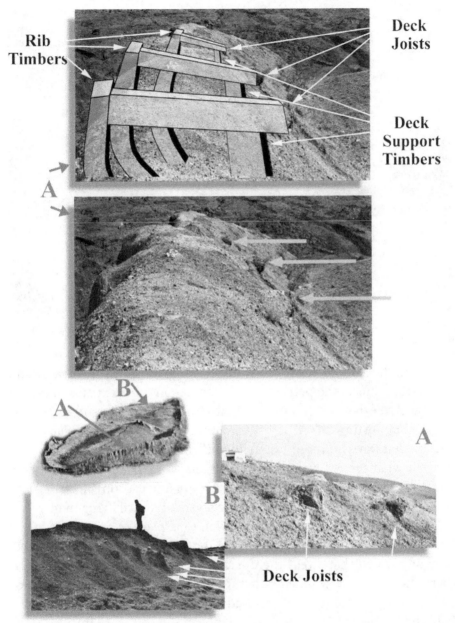

Rib Timbers

Deck Joists

Deck Support Timbers

A

A

B

A

B

A

Deck Joists

However, the deck joists, being located high on the sides of the ribs, are located in a position where the surface water flows past them. This limits the "frost wedging" to a degree, which other structures located in a lower section where the surface water tends to collect, suffer. What this means in simple language is that the petrified structure members which are near the surface are more vulnerable to fracturing into small pieces if they lie in an area where surface water stands.

Ron is standing below 2 deck joists showing where the deck broke away and collapsed downward.

In the winters, the water, which has seeped into its tiny cracks and crevasses, subjects the petrified structure to continual expansion due to the water freezing and fracturing it into pieces. Once the soil surrounding and supporting this structure is removed, the fragments collapse into a heap. You have no more visibly identifiable petrified structure, only a heap of what looks like rocks. But lab analysis still reveals what these "rocks" once were by the presence of the organic carbon which is NOT present in objects (natural rocks) which were not once living matter.

In 1939, a very unique excavation took place of an ancient burial boat known today as the "Sutton Hoo" boat. When carefully excavated, they discovered that, "yes", there had once been an ancient burial boat there- however, the wooden structure had long ago decayed. What was STILL present were the decomposed and siliconized iron fittings which held the timbers together. As they removed the soil from the area, they discovered that the decayed wood had left a color difference in the soil which distinctly showed the structure of the ship in the earth. The iron fittings, still in place, combined with this coloration in the soil, allowed the excavators to preserve the perfect imprint of the ship. On a very small scale, this is similar to the condition of the ark except for the fact that the ark does still contain a large amount of internal petrified structures.

But how do we know about the internal structure? The radar scans. The sub-surface interface radar revealed a pattern of internal structure which the makers of the radar determined to be "not of natural origin". The radar doesn't tell us precisely what the internal structure is made of, but a limited distinction is possible because of different densities. However, it definitely reveals its shape and location. And whatever it is, the specialists declared that it is "man-made" because of its organized pattern. Nothing in nature occurs in the perfect pattern of a ship's internal structure.

This, combined with the pattern of evenly-spaced metal detector readings on the ship, prove that the structure contained metal at the intersections where the timbers were joined together. The "rocks" which displayed the metal readings may have looked like "rocks", but we now understand why. The timbers which contained the metal fittings were fossilized. When exposed to the elements, they fragmented which left them looking like weathered rocks. But, the metal content is so concentrated at these precise spots that lab analyses reveal the presence of metal in concentrations and forms which is not found in nature.

Above- Ron with the ark model he constructed from the accumulated data.

Right- The 15 foot model he built in a Nashville lake.

Noah's Ark and the Visitors Center in 1992.

Ron in 1989 with the Visitors Center and the ark viewed from a different angle.

6

WHY IS NOAH'S ARK REVEALED NOW?

As evidenced throughout the Bible, God presents different truths to His people at different times depending on our needs. Unfortunately for most of us, we are not aware of how badly we are in need of a true connection with our Lord, of a daily living experience with Him.

We have no way of comparing our present spiritual situation with that of the peoples of past history except by a study of the history of our world and to read and know the Bible. Many of us suffer from the delusion that we are doing great compared to those around us. Satan has really pulled the wool over our eyes as to the real truth, for like Solomon, our apostasy has been gradual. The insidious poison of evil has blinded us.

"For we dare not make ourselves of the number, or compare ourselves with some that commend themselves: but they measuring themselves by themselves, and comparing themselves among themselves, are not wise." II Corinthians 10:12.

All through history, the true Christians were persecuted, tortured and even martyred because of their faith. The hatred that led to Christ's crucifixion would continue to burn in the heart of the world against all who were His followers. Beginning with Nero, Christians were accused of horrible crimes. Some were then crucified, some were ripped apart by wild animals in arenas, and thousands were burned alive while tied atop tall poles in Nero's courtyard.

For hundreds of years Christians were pursued as beasts of prey and had to hide. Yet in spite of this, Christianity flourished. Realizing that he couldn't victor over Christ by the killing of the body, Satan implemented a new plan.

In 313 A.D., Constantine decreed Christianity to be the official religion of the empire. While the persecutions ceased, this set the stage for the deterioration of the church. At this time, most of the people were heathens, and in order to make Christianity appealing to the heathens, their practices were incorporated into the church. They had their priests, altars and sacrifices, and soon so did the church. Their superstitions and magical objects were transformed into the veneration of the relics of the martyrs and saints. Christianity was nothing more than a new name for their heathen worship. The worst part was that it became difficult for the true Christian to see the truth through the deceptions.

Before long, the church began to persecute the heretics and "heathens." Once again, the true Christians faced persecution. And throughout the ages until our present day, the church has deteriorated through Satan's devices.

Paul tells us that *"all that will live godly in Christ Jesus shall suffer persecution."* II Timothy 3:12. As long as there was persecution, the church remained relatively steadfast and pure. But the church as a whole today is so tainted as to be virtually devoid of true religion. The great struggle now is not to escape death or martyrdom as a result of our faith, but to see the truth through the deceptions. Paul saw these things creeping into the church even in his day as he wrote, *"the mystery of iniquity doth already work."* II Thessalonians 2:7.

The early history of our country reveals how vital our forefathers' dependence on God was. When man has nothing, when he has to till the soil and live off the fruits of his own labor, if he has faith in God, he can see His power in his daily life. But as we progressed, an evil pattern began to emerge.

As power struggles develop and men discover that through their power they can benefit from the labors of others, the time inevitably comes that a choice must be made. These men must choose between God and their own devices. As they decide, greed, love of pleasure and ease step in. Satan whispers in their ear that God only forbids things because He knows you can be like Him, that He wants to keep you in ignorance, the same lie he deceived Eve with. The same lie of the "new age" movement - that we can "tap in" to God's wisdom because after all, we're all a part of Him and therefore, are Him. An easy pill to swallow for those looking for a way out.

But look at slavery of our own not-too-distant past. Man soon learns to rationalize his every action against the inner-promptings which tell him right from wrong. Like a callous which forms from repeated abuse, the heart becomes hardened, at first unwilling and finally unable

68

to hear and accept the truth.

"*Thy princes are rebellious, and companions of thieves: everyone loveth gifts and followeth after rewards: they judge not the fatherless, neither does the cause of the widow come unto them.*" Isaiah 1:23.

There can be no doubt that Christ will soon return for His children. I cannot present the evidences God has preserved for us in these last days without presenting them for what they are - a chance for us to see the absolute truth as recorded in the Bible and evidences of God's past judgments.

Paul said "*Moreover, brethren, I would not that ye should be ignorant, how that all our fathers were under the cloud, and passed through the sea; And all were baptized unto Moses in the cloud and in the sea.*" I Corinthians 10:1,2.

Timothy wrote for us the following warning, given by the Holy Spirit, that we would be aware of the seriousness and dangers we'd face: "*Now the Spirit speaketh expressly, that in the latter times some shall depart from the faith, giving heed to seducing spirits, and doctrines of devils; Speaking lies in hypocrisy;*" I Timothy 4:1,2.

"*This know also, that in the last days perilous times shall come. For men shall be lovers of their own selves, covetous, boasters, proud, blasphemers, disobedient to parents, unthankful, unholy, Without natural affection, trucebreakers, false accusers, incontinent, fierce, despisers of those that are good, Traitors, heady, highminded, lovers of pleasures more than lovers of God; Having a form of godliness, but denying the power thereof: from such turn away.*" II Timothy 3:1-5. We are told in no uncertain terms to "preach the Word", "*For the time will come when they will not endure sound doctrine; but after their own lusts shall they heap to themselves teachers, having itching ears; And they shall turn away their ears from the truth, and shall be turned unto fables.*" II Timothy 4:3-4.

We would have to be blind not to see that the days of which are written here are the days we are living in. While Thomas didn't believe until he could see in His hands the print of the nails, Christ offered him this evidence. He didn't condemn Thomas because he didn't believe until he saw, for He said, "*Reach hither thy finger, and behold My hands; and reach hither thy hand and thrust it into My side: and be not faithless, but believing. And Thomas answered and said unto Him, My Lord and my God. Jesus saith unto him, Thomas, because thou hast seen me, thou hast believed: blessed are they that have not seen, and yet have believed.*" John 20:27-29.

69

God desires that all men be saved. All through the Bible, we read of the mighty works of His Hand; how He gave His children all the evidence we could imagine, that they should believe. Now He is preparing the way for new evidences, preserved by Him thousands of years ago for revealing in His time. Only today do we need "proof" that Noah really survived the flood. Only today do we find it impossible to believe God parted the Red Sea so Moses and the Israelites could cross on dry land. *"Beware lest any man spoil you through philosophy and vain deceit, after the tradition of men, after the rudiments of the world, and not after Christ."* Colossians 2:8.

Is this world really ready for Christ's return? Revelation describes the terrible condition of the religious world right before the end. And Revelation 12:12 tells us how Satan is going to have great wrath *"because he knoweth that he hath but a short time."*

If this is the time of the end, we cannot deny the terrible state of the world. If we can't see it, it's because Satan has blinded us. But, *"... As I live, saith the Lord God, I have no pleasure in the death of the wicked; but that the wicked turn from his way and live:"* Ezekiel 33:11. *"And it shall come to pass in the last days, saith God, I will pour out of My Spirit upon all flesh:"* Acts 2:17. God is going to bring this world to a close with a tremendous show of His power.

Right before the end, Revelation 18:1 states *"And after these things I saw another angel come down from heaven, having great power; and the earth was lightened with his glory."* Then this angel cries out to us, *"Babylon the great is fallen, is fallen, and is become the habitation of devils and the hold of every foul spirit, and a cage of every unclean and hateful bird."*

He's giving you proof that His judgments are real; that His Word is divinely inspired and accurate right down to every jot and tittle. It's going to be up to you to accept the truth in your heart or reject it and listen to men who, as agents of Satan, will try to discredit God's work.

" *And, behold, I come quickly; and my reward is with me, to give to every man according as his work shall be.".. "I am Alpha and Omega, the beginning and the end, the first and the last."*

"I Jesus have sent mine angel to testify unto you these things in the churches. I am the root and the offspring of David, and the bright and morning star." Revelation. 22:12,13,16

7

MY TESTIMONY

The following experiences are highlights of my personal relationship with our wonderful and caring Lord. Before God, who cannot lie and to whom lying lips are an abomination, I present these experiences to you as real and the substance of my deep love and humble gratitude to Him, Who with His Son *"freely gives us all things."* Romans 8:32, and who *"is able to do exceeding abundantly above all that we ask or think,..."* Ephesians 3:20.

As I became aware of the reality of God, I prayed that if it was not asking too much, He would allow me to have a dream in which I could see the earth restored or perhaps even heaven. Several years later, after I had prayed for this three or four times and had become convinced it wasn't His will, I had a vivid, technicolor dream; I was floating noiselessly through the air above a body of crystal clear water. The water appeared to be alive with multicolored and variously shaped fish and other creatures. Then, I looked up and all around and saw mounds of grass and flower-covered earth protruding from the water. On each of the mounds grew a massive tree whose amazingly long, low branches spread out in all directions and touched the tips of identical branches extending from similar trees on the numerous other mounds. The leaves and branches seemed alive with breathtakingly colored birds and butterflies.

After a while, I became aware of the silence, the absence of any "motor" noise, and suddenly wondered what was propelling me up and over the water. Looking up, down and all around, I saw that I was simply floating through the air. I then looked ahead and saw that the water ended in a profusion of breathtaking flowering vegetation that included lilies, cattails and many others unfamiliar to me. Beyond these, a luxurious, multicolored valley with predominantly green and yellow vegetation swept away from me and upward to dark green hued mountains. I awoke and immediately thanked our Heavenly Father for His kindness in answering a sinner's prayer.

After this first dream and well into the hectic events involving Noah's Ark, the Red Sea crossing, how Joseph built the Step Pyramid for the pharaoh of the seven year famine, the site of the real Mt. Sinai, several seasons of excavation that led to the discovery of the Ark of the Covenant and several other startling evidences of the crucifixion site, I was struck with a deep depression. Being aware of how God had miraculously helped me locate the remains of evidences and artifacts from most major events of the Bible, I was struck with the impossibility of my being able to handle the complicated business of getting the facts out to the people along with the significance of each discovery in the end times of earth's history.

In a state of abject discouragement, I fell asleep and again, dreamed. In this dream, I was in some unknown location high upon a ledge or something where it was possible to look out and see the entire world with its cities, seas and people. The people were scurrying about like millions of ants on an anthill. For some reason, I looked about for a means to get to the highest point from which I might shout and hopefully get some of their attention. To my left and high up on the side of a nearly sheer cliff face was a narrow ledge. Without hesitation, I decided to attempt to climb the cliff to the ledge. The loose stones and rocks under my feet began to slip and slide as I climbed. After what seemed like an eternity, I finally reached the ledge, pulled myself up carefully and turned around. I shouted "JESUS IS COMING!" The loudness and intonation sounded exactly right to me.

Suddenly, everyone stopped scurrying about and stood looking right at me! Then, gradually the frenzied activity began again, and the greater part of the people passed from my view. All that was left were a few small groups and individuals who continued to stand and watch. The dream ended, and upon awaking I realized that God adds whatever is necessary to our own feeble efforts to accomplish His purpose. I also was deeply impressed with the reality that while God's last message would be heard and understood by all, only a relative few would "love" the truth; *"And with all deceivableness of unrighteousness in them that perish; because they received not the love of the truth, that they might be saved."* II Thessalonians 2:10. The majority would love and believe lies and therefore be lost.

"And as it was in the days of Noe, so shall it be also in the days of the Son of man." Luke 17:26.

As was my custom, in the early hours of December 22, 1980, I asked God for the privilege of witnessing to someone whom He knew to be ready to be witnessed to. I prayed that He would have me to say

72

exactly what they needed to hear. I further prayed for the privilege of helping someone that was in real need. I have discovered that I am mostly unable to distinguish between those who are truly needy and those who are "professional beggars."

After this prayer, I was strongly impressed to drive to Columbia, Kentucky, a town that was a good two and one half hours drive in good weather. However, the night before, a blizzard had hit Nashville, Tennessee, where I lived, and every road in and out of town was closed. I was on duty at Donelson Hospital for "in- house" O.B. anesthesia administration and wasn't too sure if my relief would be able to make it in. I silently prayed that when I called the state police office to check on the roads, if they said all the roads were closed, I wouldn't go. I called. Their reply was "unless it is a life or death situation, stay off the roads." I knew without hesitation that I was to go. Not knowing what I was to do or who it would be for, I brought along three copies of a book I found to be a marvelous presentation of the plan of salvation, and my small, marked Bible and set out.

I only saw four cars along the approximate 120 mile drive. Two of these were stopped in the middle of the road; one was a motorist with a wheel broken from his car and the other was a highway patrolman helping this motorist. My 1976 Dodge Maxi Van had chronic fan belt problems with a great deal of overheating problems.

After several long hours of miserable driving, I arrived in Columbia. The slippery road conditions convinced me of my need for a set of studded snow tires on the back of the van, so I pulled into the Columbia Tire Shop, bought a set and had them mounted. Still not having any idea who I was to witness to, I struck up a conversation with the owner of the shop. We discussed world events and some religious subjects, but the encounter didn't seem to warrant such a difficult trip through ice and snow. So, just in case this was why I had been sent here, I gave him one of the copies of the books, "The Story of Redemption", I had brought. He thanked me for the book, I paid for the tires and left.

What now? Where was I to go? I decided that a cup of hot coffee would feel mighty good right then, so I pulled into a restaurant. I chatted with the waitress. Again the topics were world events and a little on religious subjects, but I doubted this was the encounter God had lined up; I gave her a copy of the book just in case. It began to get dark, and the return trip to Nashville began to weigh heavily on my mind. I believed the purpose of my trip hadn't been accomplished, but with the long, cold

73

trip ahead and the absence of a single clue as to my mission, I decided to finish my coffee and be on my way.

I paid my tab and got in my van. The parking lot tilted toward the street, and I figured it would be easy to get out of the snow there. It started o.k., but as I attempted to back out, the tires spun and slipped to the side. It wouldn't budge. I got out to see what the problem was. After living in Michigan for many years, I usually had no problem getting myself or others around in the snow and getting "stuck" vehicles out of ditches. As I carefully examined the van, I knew there was no earthly reason for the van to be stuck.

After spending about 30 minutes trying to get out, I gave up and went in for some soup and coffee to warm me up. Embarrassed, I sat down and ordered. People came over and offered to help me, but in my humiliation I said "thanks" and just sat a while and ate. Secretly, deep down inside, down where we all live, I began to resent the whole day's business, especially the humiliation of not being able to get in the van and drive out like the few others who came and went while I sat. For forty-five minutes I sat there, my resentment secretly smoldering, when I received a very strong impression to get in the van and go home. I felt a twinge of guilt over my attitude, but not knowing what else to do, I went to the van, started the engine and backed out into the street as if nothing had ever happened. I headed in the direction of the interstate that would take me home.

As I drove carefully along the west-bound lane of the toll road, my conscience began to trouble me more. There wasn't anything I could do except go back and try again, however it would have been illegal to drive back to the exit on the wrong side of the highway, and the next exit was 22 miles west. I began to pray that God would forgive me for my willfulness and please not let someone go without what He had wanted me to do just because I was a jerk.

Suddenly, from the median of the toll road staggered a dark form, falling and struggling to get to the side I was travelling on. Slowing down to see if it was a hurt animal, I realized it was a person. With a feeble wave of one arm, he signaled me to stop.

Unable to stop quickly on the snow and ice, I had to slowly back up to where he was. I swung open the passenger door and told him to get in. He was badly frozen; his hands and arms were blue up to where they disappeared into the sleeves of his lightweight coat. The point of his chin, his eyebrows, the tips of his ears and nose were white, indicating near frostbite.

As I helped him climb into the van, I asked him what he was doing out there without a car. His speech slurred; I at first thought him to be drunk, but I remembered that extreme cold thickens the tongue and slurs the speech. He slowly raised his arm and pointed to the median; he had a car was what he was trying to say. Jumping out of the van, I crossed to where he had pointed and sure enough, buried deep in the snow, sat a red compact car. I returned to the van and told him I'd take him to the next exit and he could get a wrecker to tow it out. I could tell this distressed him.

"Please, mister, help me get it out; it's three days until Christmas, and twenty-three dollars is every penny I have in this world! I need it for my wife and children's Christmas."

"There's no way we can get it out of there," I told him. "And I don't have a chain or shovel."

"Would you please just try?" he pleaded.

He had a chain in the trunk of his car and thought maybe I could pull him out with it. Totally forgotten was the reason for my trip and the guilt at my apparent failure. Still uncomfortably cold from the day's activities, I waded through the snow to where his car was all but buried. Clearing the snow from the top and sides, I opened the trunk and retrieved the chain. Digging the snow from beneath the back of the car, I securely fastened the chain around the back axle and stretched the free end to the edge of the road. It just barely reached to where I could secure it to the trailer hitch on the van after maneuvering it to that edge of the road. This accomplished, I silently prayed, "Father, if you want this car out of the snow, You are going to have to do it; I sure can't."

At that exact moment, down the east lane of the road, which had been entirely free of traffic during my trip, appeared the headlights of two cars.

"Where did they come from?", the man echoed my surprise. Maybe we had been too busy to notice, but we both thought it strange, for the headlights of two cars are not easy to miss in the dark of a snow-covered landscape such as this.

The two cars slowed to a stop; there was no need for them to pull over to the side as there was no traffic. Four husky young men got out of each car.

"Can we help you?" one of them asked in a friendly tone.

"Yes; please!" we both resounded.

There were no women, no children or older men in either car; just the eight young men. Strange, I thought, but we couldn't ask for better help. The men waded to the car, placed their hands upon it and signaled for me to pull with the van. Within seconds, the car was up on the road.

"A piece of cake," someone said.

"Thank you, thank you." we both said.

"You are welcome," we heard as the young men headed back to their cars, brushed the snow from their clothing and got in. They drove off to the east and, puzzled about missing their approach, I watched them leave. As they approached a dip in the highway, the cars slowly disappeared from sight. However, they never arose from that dip. There was no exit for at least two miles, and they hadn't turned around- they had simply vanished into thin air. I remembered Psalms 34:7 as I silently thanked our Father, *"The angel of the Lord encampeth round about them that fear Him, and delivereth them."*

I cleared the snow from his engine, especially from around the spark plugs and ignition wires. I got in, and it started easily. After a short test drive, I left the motor running, got out and climbed into the van where the man was sitting. I told him it was ready and I would follow him to the next exit.

"My hands won't work. Do you mind if I warm up a little while longer?"

"Of course," I replied. To save his gas, I got out and turned off his car, returned to the van and commented on what good fortune we had had.

"Do you believe in God, mister?" he asked me with almost pleading eyes.

Over an hour later, we had reviewed all the Bible texts on all his questions. I read to him with my fingers moving along the text so he could read along also. Finally, he briskly wiggled his fingers and said he was ready to go.

"Would you mind if I say a little prayer for you before you go?" I asked.

"Please,... please do." he said.

I prayed for him and his family and thanked God for helping us get his car out. When I opened my eyes, he was crying. With tears rolling down his face, he told me this was the best Christmas of his entire life. He explained how he drove the toll road every weekend to and from his work and how today as he returned home he had been driving along wonder-

76

ing if there was anything to God, religion and the Bible. Then, without warning, his car had just swerved into the snow bank down inside the median. After two hours of waiting, no one had come along, and he had finally decided he was going to die right there in the snow. He told me how he prayed that if God was real, that He please take care of his family. Now, he knew for certain; God was real.

He asked me how he could explain all of this to his family, and I gave him my last copy of "The Story of Redemption." Suddenly, I realized what this trip had been all about.

Another time when I prayed the witnessing prayer was as I was returning from a weekend of continuing education classes in Williamsburg, Virginia. Driving along Interstate 81/VA and enjoying the beautiful scenery, I suddenly noticed my fuel gauge sitting on empty. I decided to pull into the right hand lane and get off at the next exit to "gas up".

I passed a sign that said "Next Exit - 3 Miles". After I moved into the right lane, I found there were three cars ahead of me, all travelling about 45 miles per hour, so I decided I had plenty of time to pass them and still get back into the right hand lane to exit. When I pulled out to pass, the middle of the three cars pulled out in front of me and sped up even with the first car and held that position. Then, the third car pulled up even with me. I wouldn't have believed it was possible for a driver, who wanted to exit an interstate with two miles to maneuver before the exit, to get boxed in where it was impossible for him to make his exit without risking an accident. But I know first hand, now it is.

As we crept past the exit, I breathed a prayer that the Lord would keep me from running out of fuel before the next exit, which was 11 miles ahead. Anxiously, I watched the gauge and soon found myself pulling into a gas station on the next exit. After I filled up with gas, I noticed a Kroger store a few blocks away and decided to pick up some snacks and a drink so I wouldn't have to stop again for lunch. En route to the store, I noticed a "used book and clothing" store just opposite one of the entrances. I felt a strong impression to go in. However, the last thing in the world I needed was more used books or clothing, so I headed to Kroger and got my snacks. As I left though, I again felt a very strong impression to go in.

As I walked in and looked around, I saw a G.E.D. study guide that would be useful the next time someone asked for help with their G.E.D. test. Then I saw a blue jean jacket that looked like it would fit one of my kids. The place had been quite busy when I entered it, but as I went to check out, I noticed it had emptied. I assumed that the store manager was who I was to witness to as he and a lady, whom I later learned was his wife, were the sole occupants in the store.

Not knowing how to start any meaningful conversation, I looked about for something to start talking about. As I paid for my items, my eye fell upon a nice collection of arrowheads in the glass case beneath the cash register.

Three hours later, I had shown him, his wife and young son, who later arrived from school, how Joseph had built the first pyramid, answered many questions they had about religion and was asking if it would be alright if I said a little prayer with them before I left. I prayed a simple, direct prayer for their health, happiness and especially for their salvation.

Opening my eyes, I saw tears streaming down all three of their faces. The husband and father, in a trembling voice, explained how he had been in church all of his life, was an elder and greeted members at the door of his church, but until that day he hadn't really known that God and His salvation was a reality.

The joy of going on God's errands is addicting. If I have not experienced a "divine encounter" for more than a week, I go into a state of depression and prayerfully seek out what has made me useless to God and His work. He, in mercy, always makes me aware of the problem, helps me straighten it out and puts me back to work. Friends, don't settle for a pretended relationship with God. You can and must find the real thing.

One last experience I want to share. In August of 1978, my two sons and I had the thrill of a lifetime. After a brief research on the site at which the ancient Egyptian army drowned while pursuing Moses and the children of Israel, we decided to go to Egypt and check it out. We found the site, and after a crash course in scuba diving right before we left home, we were able to photograph the remains of three chariots on the sea floor.

We then hurried home, gathered some equipment that would enable us to bring some of these artifacts to the surface and went to Giza. There we met with and explained to Mr. Nassef Mohamed Hassan, the Director of Antiquities for the Giza/Saqqara District and who later became the Director of the Egyptian Department of Antiquities, how the pyramids were built and gave him a short paper with diagrams for the machines and methods. We left, Mr. Hassan happily studying our paper, and us, with our permission to retrieve some artifacts to bring to him for evaluation.

We headed back to the site and began diving. While I was swimming underwater at about a 30 foot depth, marking possible candidates for retrieval from among several skeletal and chariot remains, I got severely sunburned. I, foolishly, didn't realize this could happen, and my feet swelled to the point that I couldn't get into my diving equipment. We were devastated. There was nothing for us to do except travel to Jerusalem and wait for our A.P.E.X. flight home, nurse my burns and possibly return to Egypt and finish the project.

Arriving in Jerusalem, we settled into a very uncomfortable but very cheap youth hostel. We did some sight-seeing, read a lot and in general had a miserable time. One day, I decided to visit the Garden Tomb. That was to be a place and experience never to be forgotten.

Inside the shop, I visited with the people who ran it and shared the discovery of Noah's Ark, how Joseph built the pyramids and showed them the photographs of the chariot parts from the Red Sea crossing site. They in turn asked me to stay during the two and a half hour closing time from 12:00 noon until 2:30 p.m. and look the Garden Tomb area over for possible archaeological remains. Returning to the hostel, I told my boys of my plans, and they decided to stay there and read. So, I returned to the Garden Tomb.

While looking through the gift shop for some books, I noticed a red haired man that looked like he had helped hang his last friend. I spoke to him cheerfully, discovered him to be an American, chatted briefly, wished him a good day and walked into the garden area that was to close very shortly. I was examining a site where some ancient coins had been found when I became aware that someone was standing behind me.

Turning around, I saw the red haired gentleman. He inquired as to what I was doing. After a brief explanation, he said, "You are a scientist; do you believe in God and the Bible?" Two and a half hours later, after answering his questions and showing him the answers in the Bible, I asked him if I could pray with him. He said, "yes," and when I opened my eyes, tears were just streaming down his face.

"God sent you to me," he said. He explained how he was a pastor and had been deeply and persistently impressed to come to Jerusalem and convert the Jews. He'd prayed for signs and gotten positive ones. He went on to explain that he had gotten the promise of the assistant pastorship at the only Baptist Church in Jerusalem but lost it when the previous one decided to stay at the last minute, after he and his family had sold their home and belongings and already arrived in Jerusalem. He told me how he had looked for work everywhere but could find none and how he'd borrowed money to send his family home.

Just that morning, he'd gone to Haifa to ship their few personal belongings home and taken the bus back to Jerusalem. When he arrived back here, he said he'd felt a strong impression, which he was now inclined to ignore since his previous impressions had resulted in his situation, but nonetheless he decided to walk the 42 blocks and had just arrived when I saw him in the gift shop. He'd asked the kind folks there if he could be allowed to stay there during the two and a half hour "closed" period, and they said o.k. Now, as the tears were still streaming, he said that now, for the first time in all his years as a minister, he had a saving message to preach.

I, in my disappointment at not being able to retrieve the chariot parts, asked him, "Why, since you are from Little Rock and I'm from Nashville, couldn't we have met maybe in Memphis or at least somewhere closer to home?"

"If you had known me before this experience, you would not have asked that question. I knew everything and wouldn't have listened to you or anyone else," was his reply.

Then, I shared with him my reason for being in the Middle East and my keen disappointment at not being able to complete what I had set out to do at the Red Sea. He then, assuming his role as a pastor and new friend, assured me that God had better plans than we had and would bring them about in good time. And if we were teachable, he would use us. The Spirit moved greatly within the both of us, and at this, we both went our separate ways of service, rejoicing in our loving God.

When we experience divine encounters, we can be sure that those we witness to will ultimately be saved and, in most cases, become effective witnesses themselves, the thief on the cross being one of the few exceptions to this. But this is only possible if we allow God to use us in His work.

The unspeakable joy of knowing with certainty that you are where God wants you to be, doing exactly what He wants you to do, can be yours. And then, one day, the unspeakable joy of seeing your family and others you have helped lead to Christ, walking the streets of gold, eating of the tree of life and drinking from the river of life eternally, will also be yours.

THE WITNESSING PRAYER

I have shared with you my addiction to "divine appointments". God, in His mercy, has invited us sinners (in rehabilitation) to bear faithful witness to Him, His character and salvation. You, with me, can be certain that you are in His will by taking three simple steps:

1) Ask God, in Christ's name, to forgive and cleanse you of every sin that separates you from His will.

2) Pray the "witnessing prayer", that you may be honored of Him by being led by His Spirit to bear effective, saving witness and/or help someone for whom Christ died.

3) When He provides the divine appointment, be totally honest and truthful with whoever you witness to or help. There are a vast number out there who have and are bearing a false witness, but rationalize that they are doing God and mankind a service by "embellishing" the truth, making it more spectacular or "punching it up". The extreme end of allowing Satan to lead you in this falsification of the facts is to become a destroyer of yourself, your family and others. God cannot lie. When we do, even if we "do it for a good reason", we separate ourselves from the only saving source of power in the universe.

Effective divine encounters are reconfirmations from God that we are in His will. Attacks by Satan and his hosts, both human and demonic, are another reconfirmation of our walk with God. No attacks means we're doing Satan's will, not God's.

Even Paul knew the real enemy for he said, *"Wherefore we would have come unto you, even I Paul, once and again; but Satan hindered us."* I Thessalonians 2:18.

So friends, be aware. The Word of God is not an idle tale when we are warned, *"Be sober, be vigilant; because your adversary the devil, as a roaring lion, walketh about, seeking whom he may devour:"* I Peter 5:8.

Don't believe those who tell you that if you are a true Christian, you won't have problems and everyone will love you. For that's a lie. Satan will disguise his evil and use as his agents those who are not Christians, though they may profess to be. *"Marvel not, my brethren, if the world hate you."* I John 3:13.

But remember His promise, in the words of Christ Himself, *"And ye shall be hated of all men for my name's sake: but he that endureth to the end shall be saved."* Matthew 10:22.

Again, our choices are to either work for God, share and enjoy His salvation throughout eternity, or to fall into the grasp of a merciless demon, and share total and eternal destruction in the hell-fires which will destroy Satan and his evil angels; the same fire God uses to purify this world of the last vestiges of sin and sinners before He restores it to its Edenic beauty and makes it the eternal home of the *"nations of them which are saved..."* Revelation 21:24.

8

Last Message
Only God is Immortal- Man is NOT

1TI 6:14 ... *our Lord Jesus Christ: 15 Which in his times he shall shew, who is the blessed and only Potentate, the King of kings, and Lord of lords; 16 Who only hath immortality, dwelling in the light which no man can approach unto; whom no man hath seen, nor can see: to whom be honour and power everlasting. Amen.*

JOB 14:14 *If a man die, shall he live again? all the days of my appointed time will I wait, till my change come. 15 Thou shalt call, and I will answer thee: thou wilt have a desire to the work of thine hands.... 19:25 For I know that my redeemer liveth, and that he shall stand at the latter day upon the earth: 26 And though after my skin worms destroy this body, yet in my flesh shall I see God:*

ECC 9:10 *Whatsoever thy hand findeth to do, do it with thy might; for there is no work, nor device, nor knowledge, nor wisdom, in the grave, whither thou goest.*

PSA 146:4 *His breath goeth forth, he returneth to his earth; in that very day his thoughts perish.*

EZE 18:4 *Behold, all souls are mine; as the soul of the father, so also the soul of the son is mine: the soul that sinneth, it shall die.... 20 ...The son shall not bear the iniquity of the father, neither shall the father bear the iniquity of the son: the righteousness of the righteous shall be upon him, and the wickedness of the wicked shall be upon him.*

The Tree of Life- Necessary for Eternal Life

GEN 1:26 *And God said, Let us make man in our image, after our likeness: and let them have dominion over the fish of the sea, and over the fowl of the air, and over the cattle, and over all the earth, and over every creeping thing that creepeth upon the earth.... 2:16 And the LORD God commanded the man, saying, Of every tree of the garden thou mayest freely eat: 17 But of the tree of the knowledge of good and evil, thou shalt not eat of it: for in the day that thou eatest thereof thou shalt surely die.*

GEN 3:22 And the LORD God said, Behold, the man is become as one of us, to know good and evil: and now, lest he put forth his hand, and take also of the tree of life, and eat, and live for ever: 23 Therefore the LORD God sent him forth from the garden of Eden, to till the ground from whence he was taken. 24 So he drove out the man; and he placed at the east of the garden of Eden Cherubims, and a flaming sword which turned every way, to keep the way of the tree of life.

Adam and Eve were mortal but had access to the tree of life. When Adam sinned, he and Eve were barred from the Garden of Eden and the tree of life. From that moment on:

HEB 9:27 ... it is appointed unto men once to die, but after this the judgment.

Through Christ, means were provided to give mankind the gift of eternal life:

REV 22:14 Blessed are they that do his commandments, that they may have right to the tree of life, and may enter in through the gates into the city.

The FIRST Deception- that Man is Immortal

GEN 3:4 And the serpent said unto the woman, Ye shall not surely die: This lie by Satan caused Adam and Eve's fall. It has caused the destruction of billions down through the ages, and will yet bring about the destruction of billions now living upon the earth. God has said:

ECC 9:5 For the living know that they shall die: but the dead know not any thing, neither have they any more a reward; for the memory of them is forgotten. 6 Also their love, and their hatred, and their envy, is now perished; neither have they any more a portion for ever in any thing that is done under the sun.... 10 Whatsoever thy hand findeth to do, do it with thy might; for there is no work, nor device, nor knowledge, nor wisdom, in the grave, whither thou goest.

JOB 14:14 If a man die, shall he live again? all the days of my appointed time will I wait, till my change come. 15 Thou shalt call, and I will answer thee: thou wilt have a desire to the work of thine hands... 20 Thou prevailest for ever against him, and he passeth: thou changest his countenance, and sendest him away. 21 His sons come to honour, and he knoweth it not; and they are brought low, but he perceiveth it not of them.

JOB 19:25 *For I know that my redeemer liveth, and that he shall stand at the latter day upon the earth: 26 And though after my skin worms destroy this body, yet in my flesh shall I see God: 27 Whom I shall see for myself, and mine eyes shall behold, and not another; though my reins be consumed within me.*

THESE STATEMENTS CLEARLY INFORM US THAT THE SOUL AND BODY ARE UNCONSCIOUS DURING DEATH. Remember, God never alters the thing that has gone out of His lips- *(PSA 89:34 My covenant will I not break, NOR ALTER THE THING THAT HAS GONE OUT OF MY LIPS.)* Keeping this in mind we need not be confused by what Paul (by divine inspiration) says in:

2CO 5:8 *We are confident, I say, and willing rather to be absent from the body, and to be present with the Lord.*

When a Christian (in word and deed) dies, their next conscious moment will be at the resurrection of the just.

1TH 4:15 *For this we say unto you by the word of the Lord, that we which are alive and remain unto the coming of the Lord shall not prevent them which are asleep. 16 For the Lord himself shall descend from heaven with a shout, with the voice of the archangel, and with the trump of God: and the dead in Christ shall rise first: 17 Then we which are alive and remain shall be caught up together with them in the clouds, to meet the Lord in the air: and so shall we ever be with the Lord. 18 Wherefore comfort one another with these words.*

This unawareness of the passage of time is demonstrated by people who have been in coma from a head injury, or any one of who have gone to sleep tired and been awakened in what seamed to us seconds but was in fact several hours. Also, people who are anesthetized for surgery have no awareness of the passage of time, if well anesthetized.

Remember- God never alters the thing that has gone out of His lips.

REV 16:13 *And I saw three unclean spirits like frogs come out of the mouth of the dragon, and out of the mouth of the beast, and out of the mouth of the false prophet. 14 For they are the spirits of devils, working miracles, which go forth unto the kings of the earth and of the whole world, to gather them to the battle of that great day of God Almighty.*

REV 3:10 *Because thou hast kept the word of my patience, I also will keep thee from the hour of temptation, which shall come upon all the world, to try them that dwell upon the earth. 11 Behold, I come quickly: hold that fast which thou hast, that no man take thy crown.*

Dangerous to Believe in "Life After Death" or Immortality of the Soul!

WHY IS A CLEAR UNDERSTANDING OF THE STATE OF THE DEAD IMPORTANT TO US AT THIS TIME? Angels both good and bad are able to appear as people. They can appear as our dead family members or other loved ones, or famous people or whoever they wish to impersonate. And since they have been here since the time of Adam and Eve, they know every detail of the lives of those long ago deceased, and can communicate those details, which convinces many people that they truly are the "spirits of the dead". We must know that the dead "know not any thing"; otherwise we can be deceived by spirits of devils posing as people. Christ and two angels appeared to Abraham and Sarah as common travelers. The two angels appeared to Lot, his family and all the men of Sodom as ordinary travelers. (See Gen Chapters 18, 19.) Satan appeared as a serpent to Eve. If we have any question about who is talking to us, God has given us a fail-proof means of telling if they are of God or of Satan:

ISA 8:20 To the law and to the testimony: if they speak not according to this word, it is because there is no light in them.

Satan will soon appear as an "angel of light"and impersonate Christ; his fallen angels will impersonate the apostles and other writers of the Bible. Satan in the guise of Christ will tell the world he has changed the law of God. Since God does not *"alter the thing that has gone out of my lips"*, this claim by Satan to have changed the law will prove that he is an imposter. The claim by his demons in the guise of Bible writers, that the Bible (God's Word) is not as they wrote it, will likewise prove them to be impostors.

2CO 11:14 And no marvel; for Satan himself is transformed into an angel of light. 15 Therefore it is no great thing if his ministers also be transformed as the ministers of righteousness; whose end shall be according to their works.

GAL 1:8 But though we, or an angel from heaven, preach any other gospel unto you than that which we have preached unto you, let him be accursed.

JUD 1:14 And Enoch also, the seventh from Adam, prophesied of these, saying, Behold, the Lord cometh with ten thousands of his saints, 15 To execute judgment upon all, and to convince all that are ungodly among them of all their ungodly deeds which they have ungodly committed, and of all their hard speaches which ungodly sinners have spoken against Him.

Unclean

GEN 3:2 *And the woman said unto the serpent, We may eat of the fruit of the trees of the garden: 3 But of the fruit of the tree which is in the midst of the garden, God hath said, Ye shall not eat of it, neither shall ye touch it, lest ye die. 4 AND THE SERPENT SAID UNTO THE WOMAN, YE SHALL NOT SURELY DIE;... 6 And when the woman saw that the tree was good for food, and that it was pleasant to the eyes, and a tree to be desired to make one wise, she took of the fruit thereof, and did eat, and gave also unto her husband with her; and he did eat.*

Satan lied to and deceived Adam and Eve about what God told them not to eat. He has an army of deceived and deceivers through whom he is deceiving this last generation of earth's inhabitants about the same thing.

2TH 2:9 *Even him, whose coming is after the working of Satan with all power and signs and lying wonders, 10 And with all deceivableness of unrighteousness in them that perish; because they received not the love of the truth, that they might be saved. 11 And for this cause God shall send them strong delusion, that they should believe a lie: 12 That they all might be damned who believed not the truth, but had pleasure in unrighteousness.*

ISA 66:15 *For, behold, the LORD will come with fire, and with his chariots like a whirlwind, to render his anger with fury, and his rebuke with flames of fire. 16 For by fire and by his sword will the LORD plead with all flesh: and the slain of the LORD shall be many. 17 They that sanctify themselves, and purify themselves in the gardens behind one tree in the midst, eating swine's flesh, and the abomination, and the mouse, shall be consumed together, saith the LORD.*

PSA 89:34 *My covenant will I not break, NOR ALTER THE THING THAT HAS GONE OUT OF MY LIPS.*

2CO 6:17 *Wherefore come out from among them, and be ye separate, saith the Lord, and touch not the unclean thing; and I will receive you,... 18 And will be a Father unto you, and ye shall be my sons and daughters, saith the Lord Almighty. 7:1 Having therefore these promises, dearly beloved, let us cleanse ourselves from all filthiness of the flesh and spirit, perfecting holiness in the fear of God.*

New testament scriptures are MISINTERPRETED by those who want to believe that God is a liar and want us to join them in the demonic belief that what God pronounced unclean no longer applies:

ACT 11:7 And I heard a voice saying unto me, Arise, Peter; slay and eat.... 10 And this was done three times: and all were drawn up again into heaven.

Satan wants us to believe that Christ died to cleanse things pronounced "UNCLEAN" by God (Lev.11;1-) Who does not "alter the things that has gone out of My lips". But what did Peter really learn from this vision?:

ACT 10:28 And he said unto them, Ye know how that it is an unlawful thing for a man that is a Jew to keep company, or come unto one of another nation; but God hath shewed me THAT I SHOULD NOT CALL ANY MAN COMMON OR UNCLEAN.

1CO 10:25 Whatsoever is sold in the shambles, that eat, asking no question for conscience sake:

Slaves were sold in the city market, or shambles. Can we really believe Paul approved of cannibalism!? NO! He was only discussing clean foods that had been offered (or dedicated) to heathen gods.

1CO 8:1 Now as touching things offered unto idols, we know that we all have knowledge. Knowledge puffeth up, but charity edifieth.

1CO 10:28 But if any man say unto you, This is offered in sacrifice unto idols, eat not for his sake that shewed it, and for conscience sake: for the earth is the Lord's, and the fulness thereof:

Do we want to let Satan and his followers trick us into eating things that will get us burned up by Christ at his coming?!

ISA 66:15 For, behold, the LORD will come with fire, and with his chariots like a whirlwind, to render his anger with fury, and his rebuke with flames of fire. 16 For by fire and by his sword will the LORD plead with all flesh: and the slain of the LORD shall be many. 17 They that sanctify themselves, and purify themselves in the gardens behind one tree in the midst, eating swine's flesh, and the abomination, and the mouse, shall be consumed together, saith the LORD.

A Warning To God's People for this Time

Many professed followers of God are distracted and paralyzed by the fears of last day events. If Satan succeeds in getting God's people to focus on these things instead of giving the last message, he has succeeded in eliminating them from God's last work. Our message is not to get people up in arms about helicopters, men in black uniforms, and the coming "new world order", etc.- our message is to be the Words of Life. The end of the world as we know it is at hand- Christ is coming soon. Eternal lives are at stake.

EZE 33:11 ...As I live, saith the Lord God, I have no pleasure in the death of the wicked; but that the wicked turn from his way and live: turn ye, turn ye from your evil ways; for why will ye die, O house of Israel?

ROM 6:23 For the wages of sin is death; but the gift of God is eternal life through Jesus Christ our Lord.

JOH 6:37 ...him that cometh to me I will in no wise cast out.

1JO 1:9 If we confess our sins, He is faithful and just to forgive us our sins, and to cleanse us from all unrighteousness.

1JO 3:3 And every man that hath this hope in him purifieth himself, even as HE is pure.

LUK 12:32 Fear not, little flock; for it is your Father's good pleasure to give you the kingdom.

CPSIA information can be obtained
at www.ICGtesting.com
Printed in the USA
LVHW052328231119
638234LV00004B/6/P

9 780578 142746